REMEMBERING THE FAITH

DATE DUE

Remembering the Faith

WHAT CHRISTIANS BELIEVE

Douglas J. Brouwer

WILLIAM B. EERDMANS PUBLISHING COMPANY
GRAND RAPIDS, MICHIGAN / CAMBRIDGE, U.K.

© 1999 Wm. B. Eerdmans Publishing Co.
255 Jefferson Ave. S.E., Grand Rapids, Michigan 49503 /
P.O. Box 163, Cambridge CB3 9PU U.K.

Printed in the United States of America

04 03 02 01 00 99   7 6 5 4 3 2 1

Library of Congress Cataloging-in-Publication Data

Brouwer, Douglas J.
Remembering the faith: what Christians believe / Douglas Brouwer.
p.   cm.
ISBN 0-8028-4621-1 (pbk.: alk. paper)
1. Theology, Doctrinal Popular works.   I. Title.
BT77.B775 1999

230 — dc21   99-28086
                                              CIP

To my congregation in Wheaton

Contents

Contents

Acknowledgments

If you had told me thirty years ago that one day I would stand in a pulpit and preach a sixteen-week sermon series on basic Christian doctrine, I would have laughed. I wasn't even interested in parish ministry at the time, and after a steady diet of doctrinal preaching in my childhood, I wasn't interested in *hearing* any more doctrinal sermons — much less preaching some of my own.

Clearly something happened to me along the way. I am happy to report that I am a parish minister and that I preach more and more doctrinal sermons as I get older. Looking back, I wish I had started even sooner. I am grateful to my parents and to the church of my childhood for equipping me in the faith. Though I couldn't have known it at the time, the faith I learned as a child has served me well as an adult. Some days I am surprised by how much of the Heidelberg Catechism I can still quote from memory.

I am also grateful to the congregations I have served along the way — in Iowa, Pennsylvania, New Jersey, and now Illinois. In different ways they have all confirmed for me my calling to be a pastor — and in particular my calling to be a preacher of the Word. In the beginning especially, when I didn't feel much like a pastor, they continued to think of me as a pastor, and slowly, miraculously, that's what I became. As I see it, I grew into the role.

Acknowledgments

I am especially grateful to my congregation in Wheaton. They listened to my sixteen-week sermon series on Christian doctrine (and my adult education series on the same themes) with such interest, appreciation, and eagerness that I began to sense there might be a strong interest in a book-length treatment of doctrinal issues. It was the interest and encouragement of my congregation in Wheaton, more than any other factor, that led me to write this book.

Early on I wanted to be a writer a lot more than I wanted to be a pastor, but God kept having other plans for me. My desire to be a writer, though, never left me. I'm not sure if I am one already, or how I'll know when I finally become one, but I work at it. I belong to a writers' group where the encouragement has always been lavish and the criticism has always been instructive. I am grateful to Michele Hempel and Patricia Locke, both gifted writers themselves, for the careful attention they paid to every word here. If this book is a good read, it's because they showed me how to make it that way.

Several people contributed in substantial ways to this book either wittingly or unwittingly. Both my brother-in-law, Marvin Hage, and my good friend, Old Testament scholar Thomas Dozeman, read the manuscript at an early stage and made many helpful suggestions. Also, Jack Roeda (the pastor of The Church of the Servant in Grand Rapids, Michigan) is a preacher I admire, and his own sermons on Christian doctrine were very helpful to me, especially in the early stages. Then there were a couple of textbooks on Christian doctrine that influenced me enormously. Shirley Guthrie's classic, *Christian Doctrine,* is a book I recommend to anyone who wants a fuller treatment of the subjects I explore here. And reading Daniel Migliore's *Faith Seeking Understanding* was a wonderful reminder of what it was like to sit in his Princeton Seminary classroom quite a few years ago. I hope I give some evidence here of having been an attentive student. Mary Hietbrink, my editor at Eerdmans, is someone I've known since our college newspaper days at Calvin College. Her encouragement and suggestions were appreciated more than she knows.

ACKNOWLEDGMENTS

Finally, I am grateful to my family — to my wife, Susan, and to my daughters, Sarah and Elizabeth. From them I have learned more than I can say about what God's grace looks like. They love me when I don't deserve it, and they show their love in countless ways. If they read this, I want them to see the words I don't say often enough to them: I love you.

God Hunger

AN INTRODUCTION

Q. 1. *What is the chief end of man?*
  A. Man's chief end is to glorify God, and to enjoy him
     forever.

Westminster Shorter Catechism, 1647

WHAT IS IT that you believe? Do you know?

Could you give an answer if you had to, if someone challenged you to say — in detail — exactly what you believed?

What is it that Christian people believe?

Over the last few years of my ministry, I have become increasingly concerned and even troubled at times about the content of the faith of the people I serve. Not *if* we believe so much as *what* we believe.

*   *   *

For the better part of a year, a member of the church I serve was in the hospital, and I would visit her there. Jane wasn't in the hospital continuously, but every time she was admitted, I would drive over and spend time with her.

Our conversations were unlike anything I have ever experienced before in the course of my ministry. I've made quite a few hospital calls over the years, but none like these. I wouldn't say that I looked forward to these visits, but I certainly didn't avoid them, either. What I felt, I suppose, was an intensity about them. By the time I left I always knew that I had been engaged, *fully* engaged. No visit with this person was ever routine.

Jane asked a lot of questions. Normally, when I go to the hospital, I'm prepared to talk about Chicago weather, or how well the Bulls are doing, or something — before gently moving into the real reason for my having "just dropped in." But this particular person had no interest in the weather or the Bulls or anything else, as far as I could determine, other than making sense of her situation, which was very serious. She knew she was going to die.

One of my seminary professors once described theology as "faith asking questions." What he meant, I think, is not that theology is a search for truth — in other words, starting out with no belief at all. Theology, as he described it, grows out of a faith that wants to know more, a faith that dares to ask questions. Faith in God is always the starting point for our questions.

2

If that's what theology is, then my friend Jane was a first-rate theologian. That's how I came to think of her. She was a person of faith who asked questions about faith, and she asked them with a depth and a persistence and an intensity that I had simply not known before my encounter with her. She wasn't content with easy or simplistic answers. Her desperate situation pushed her to explore the content of Christian faith — hers and mine.

I would walk into her room, and after the briefest of greetings she would say, "I've been reading the Bible, and I'm not sure what this statement means. What do you think?" And then she'd read it for me. Or else she'd say, "Someone said this to me last week." She would tell me what she'd heard, and then she'd say, "What do you think about that?" And our conversation would go on like that, letting up only when she was too tired to keep going. It was then that I prayed with her and said good-bye.

Q. *What is your only comfort in life and in death?*
A. That I am not my own but belong — body and soul, in life and in death — to my faithful Savior Jesus Christ.

Lord's Day 1, Heidelberg Catechism, 1563

Facing death, I would say, has a way of focusing our minds and pushing us to ask questions we might not otherwise think to ask. Facing death — or any desperate situation — has a way of putting us in touch with issues that matter. Which is one of the reasons, I believe, that some of the best theology of the last century was written around the time of World War II. When we're desperate, when we're pushed to the edge — it's at that point that we want to know the answers to ultimate questions. It's as though we say, "What is it that my faith means in light of what is happening to me or around me?"

Jane's hospital room is only one place, the most recent place, where I have felt the need to examine all of my old answers to faith's questions. Jane's final gift to me was to ask questions. Those questions helped to polish a few of the rough edges around my faith. For the last year of her life, Jane pushed me to describe my faith in some wonderfully new terms. Sometimes I did it awkwardly or haltingly, but I did it. And for that I will always be grateful to her.

My concern for the rest of us, though, is this: When we find ourselves up against life's toughest challenges, will the content of our faith be adequate to answer our questions? Do we know enough of the basics even to start asking these questions?

*   *   *

I have been a Presbyterian pastor for nearly twenty years, but I didn't grow up Presbyterian. I grew up in a strong but sometimes rigid faith tradition. I don't want to sound ungrateful about this tradition, though, because the truth is that I appreciate it more and more as I grow older. But the faith of my childhood often felt narrow and inflexible to me when I was younger. When I graduated from college and went to seminary, I heard answers there that sometimes sounded quite different from the answers I had been taught as a child.

There were times when I would go back to my dormitory room after a class, and there, all alone, I would break out in a cold sweat. I was aware that my belief system — the belief system of my childhood — had been challenged. I felt pushed and stretched in those seminary classes as I had never felt pushed and stretched before. And in those moments — it's hard to appreciate this fully because very few other degree programs (law, let's say) push people at this level (though maybe they should) — I would reach back to the content I had been taught as a child, and I would wrestle with it, trying my best to make sense of it. I would say to myself, "Okay, Doug, what *is* it that you believe?"

My belief in God was never the issue; the *content* of my faith was.

The point I want to make here is simply this: I am thankful there was something to reach back to. I am thankful there was something to lean on. I am thankful there was a content to my faith that served me well in those tough moments. The content of my faith has definitely been tempered and refined over the years — by my seminary training, for example — but the good news is that because of my early training, I have always had some wonderful raw material to work with. Sunday school, catechism classes, Christian schools, and more — I was prepared for a life of faith in a way that few people are today.

What concerns me about the people I work with today is that I often sense there is so little content to their faith, so little raw material to work with, so little to lean on when the going gets tough. I sense that people would like to ask questions about their faith but too often don't know where to begin.

Several times over the last few years I have found myself sitting at the bedside of longtime church members who are obviously dying. And though this may sound odd to you, these moments are actually some of the best parts of pastoral ministry — I mean, to be able to be with people, at those moments, at the final transitions of their lives. So often I feel blessed.

But, in the situations I have in mind now, the conversation eventually worked its way around to "What happens to us?" And what I've heard people say is, "You know, I've always thought that when we died, we just ceased to exist. When we're gone, we're gone."

The last time that happened — I don't think I'll ever forget my response — I almost shot out of my chair. I just blurted out, "But what about Easter? What did you hear on all of those Easter mornings when you were sitting in church?"

And this person said — I don't think I'll ever forget *his* response — "I don't know, but it wasn't that. I don't remember anybody saying anything about what happens to us when we die."

We went on to have a wonderful conversation, one I will always treasure, but I left his house that day thinking, "I wonder how many Easter mornings over the last twenty years I've forgotten to say what needs to be said. What exactly *is* the hope of the Christian life? Did I say it just now in a way that provided comfort and offered hope? Did I say it in a way that is consistent with my faith tradition?"

My sense is that there are Christian people who've been a part of a church for a long, long time who somehow have never heard the content of the Christian faith.

But it's not just the longtime members who concern me. I'm thinking of newer members too. What has happened over the last generation or so, according to studies I've read — and it's certainly true in my pastoral experience — is that children and young people have begun attending the church, and then, somewhere between the sixth and the eighth grade, they've dropped out. And stopped being a part of the church. So many other activities competed for their time and attention. Years later, after marriage, perhaps, or after having children, they've come back to church.

Which is wonderful. And it's awfully good to see them when they come back. But they often come back with what amounts to a sixth-grade understanding of the Christian faith — a passing acquaintance, maybe, with some of the Bible stories. They've never gone much beyond that. And as you know, you can't get very far these days with a sixth-grade education, and that's certainly true in terms of faith as well. A faith that stopped adding content in about the sixth grade is a weak and insubstantial faith. It's not going to remain standing for very long in the face of life's storms. What is there to lean on in the difficult moments of life?

What I hope to do in the chapters that follow is to describe faith in a way that adds content to it. My plan is not to argue for the truth of these beliefs. Defending the reasonableness of Christian faith is an important task, but it's not my plan here. My plan is also not to say all that can be said about these beliefs. I simply want to outline here — in a very introductory sort of way — what

Christians have always believed, the faith tradition that we've inherited. I want to whet the appetite for more reading, more reflecting. I want to do what I often do in my preaching — and that is to help people of faith get started.

In order to be people of faith who dare to ask questions — in order to be theologians — we need to know something of what other people of faith have believed and taught along the way. The Christian church has a two-thousand-year-old history of faith asking questions. If we're going to ask questions today, we should know at least something about the questions people have asked over the years — and of course the answers at which they arrived.

You cannot become smart enough to really know God. God will reveal himself to us from within. There is no need to go looking for him or call to him. He is as close as the door of your heart. He is waiting there, eager for you to open it. He wants this more than you do.

Meister Eckhart, *Sermons*

We'll call these answers to age-old questions "doctrines," or teachings. They often represent a kind of consensus that people of faith have achieved with regard to some very basic questions. Many of the church's doctrines are found in documents called catechisms, confessions, and creeds. In the chapters that follow I have included excerpts from a variety of these documents to illustrate some of the doctrines I am describing. Catechisms, confessions, and creeds all have different uses — in worship, for example, or in Christian education — but ordinarily they are an attempt to summarize what people of faith have read in the Bible or seen in the person of Jesus Christ. As we'll see, the Bible and Jesus himself are two important sources of faith content for believers.

My own faith tradition — the Reformed theological tradition — will become obvious. I make no apologies for that. It's the tradition I know best. I was steeped in it. I am biased toward it. The Reformation, made possible by people like Martin Luther and John Calvin, was an important time in the church's history. A great deal of theology has been written because of questions that people of faith dared to ask during that period of history. I am a grateful heir to this tradition. In general, though, I propose to describe the content of our faith in broad terms. People from most faith traditions should be able to recognize their questions here. My hope is to examine ideas and truths that you may have heard before, to bring them up-to-date, and to show how those ideas and truths are important today, how they may well be critical for our very survival — our *spiritual* survival.

Maybe this reference to "our very survival" sounds a little too dramatic to you. Maybe not. But this is my sense about us, based on my pastoral experience: There is an urgent need among Christian people to remember who we are and what our faith amounts to.

William Willimon teaches at Duke University, where he is also dean of the chapel. Not long ago, along with his friend Stanley Hauerwas, he wrote a little book called *Resident Aliens,* which has had quite an impact on me and many other Christian people I know. In the book he says that for hundreds of years the burden of proof, so to speak, had been on people who *didn't* believe in God. Faith was so widespread and pervasive that people who didn't believe had the task of defending themselves and explaining why they didn't.

Today, Willimon says, all of that has changed, and furthermore, the change has occurred within our lifetimes. The burden of proof has shifted. Today the dominant voice in our culture is one of unbelief, skepticism, and indifference. And so, for example, if you were to say in our culture today that you believe in a trinitarian God (as opposed to a "higher power" or an "intelligent designer"), you would have to explain what you mean. Most people today either don't believe in a trinitarian God or don't know exactly what it means to say they do. Most people today don't see the connection between their lives and doctrines as basic as the doctrine of the Trinity.

I would say that's even true of some church people. Mention "the Trinity" to some longtime church members and notice the response you get. Many of them, I'm guessing, would be hard-pressed to say why it's important for them to affirm faith in a trinitarian God.

*   *   *

So, where do we begin?

I propose that we begin where people of faith have always begun. I propose that we learn from those who have preceded us and who have thought deeply about the Christian faith.

John Calvin, in the year 1536 (when he was twenty-one years old), wrote that every human being is born with an awareness or knowledge of God. He called it an "awareness of divinity," a *sensus divinitatus*. This is different from the New Age belief that there is a little bit of God in each one of us. I hear people say that every now and then, and I'm never quite sure what that means or what it would look like. What Calvin was saying is quite different. He was saying that we are born to be in relationship with God, to give our allegiance to God. More than that, he was saying that God placed this awareness within us. Calvin always insisted that God acts first. People in my faith tradition have always maintained that God takes the initiative with us.

Some Christians like to say that "there's a God-shaped vacuum inside each one of us." Maybe you've heard that expression before. What it means, I think, is that we have been created with a yearning or hunger that will not go away until we fill it with God. Eugene Peterson, in his book *Leap Over a Wall,* writes that "God-hunger . . . is the most powerful drive in us. It's far stronger than all the drives of sex, power, security, and fame put together."

Like Peterson, Donald McCullough is a Presbyterian pastor. He puts an interesting twist on Peterson's idea in his book *The*

Trivialization of God, where he writes, "To be human is to worship. We really can't help ourselves. But what we can do is to choose the objects of our worship. We may worship God," he writes, "or we may worship any number of false gods."

We are only a fraction of your enormous creation, Lord, but we still want to praise you. You have made us for yourself, and our hearts are restless until they rest in you.

Augustine, *Confessions*

All of that certainly fits with my own experience. In response to the yearning and hunger inside us, we will do all sorts of things to satisfy ourselves. I think this explains our culture's abuse of alcohol and food and sex and even the accumulation of things. The abuse is often, I would say, a response to this hunger within — which, a person of faith would be quick to say, is actually a *spiritual* hunger.

The insidious part of it is that alcohol and food and sex and the accumulation of things seem to do the trick — for a while. They do satisfy us — in the short term. But always, I notice, the restlessness returns.

George Will once wrote a column in which he described our culture's "cult of personality." He was responding to the death of Princess Diana, but he was really describing a larger phenomenon — the need we have for objects of adulation and worship in our lives. Whether or not these people have accomplished anything truly great with their lives, Will says, now seems to be beside the point. We have the need to worship — and we will find someone or something to worship, worthy or not.

I often hear that men feel uncomfortable in Sunday morning worship. Singing the hymns, speaking the prayers — some men say that it all just feels so awkward to them. And yet, at places like the United Center during a Chicago Bulls game or at Soldier Field during a Bears game, I see and hear men hollering until they're hoarse. I holler with them. We participate in the "liturgy of game," so to speak, standing when we're asked to stand and repeating the words that are displayed on the screen. Grown men! Fully engaged in an act of worship, offering allegiance to their heroes!

It seems clear to me that Peterson and McCullough are right — to be human is to hunger for God; to be human is to want to worship. It's the choice we make that's critical. And too often, as you may have noticed, we human beings tend to opt for the lesser gods in our lives.

Over the years, people of faith have wondered about this human predisposition for the lesser gods, and the reason many give for it is sin. We weren't created to be the way we are, but our sinful nature, they say, makes it impossible for us to choose as we should. This is the human predicament.

The good news is that God doesn't leave us there.

*   *   *

One of my favorite Bible stories over the years has been the story in the book of Acts about Philip and the Ethiopian eunuch. This story became a favorite because I saw something of myself in the Ethiopian man. *His* conversion to the Christian faith was one I could relate to. The Apostle *Paul's* conversion, on the other hand, always seemed to be held up as the model or the paradigm for the way our experiences should be.

Paul, you may remember, saw a blinding light and heard a voice from heaven. In an instant, his life was changed. He had an encounter with the resurrected Christ, and he knew it. I suppose that's awfully nice when it happens, but — really — that's just not the way it is for most of us, is it? It certainly wasn't that way in my own life. Which was troubling, I have to admit, until I realized later in my life that coming to faith doesn't happen that way, *Paul's* way, for most people.

11

There is another way.

The Ethiopian man was a seeker — and, I would say, a theologian. Faith asking questions.

At some point in his life he had already found the God of Israel. Or, as I'd prefer to think of it, the God of Israel had already found him. When we meet him in this story, he is on his way back from Jerusalem, where he had worshipped in the temple. He had come a very long way to satisfy this spiritual hunger that he felt inside.

As the story begins, he is in his carriage or chariot, reading the book of Isaiah. And he is lost, as we might well be. Not geographically, but spiritually. He is uncomprehending. He isn't catching on. Just then, however, in a miracle of God's timing, Philip appears and asks him, "Do you know what you're reading?"

Relieved, the man answers, "No, as a matter of fact, I don't. Hop up here and explain it to me." Which Philip (as you know) is only too happy to do. Apparently the explanation is a good one, too, because the Ethiopian man hears the story and exclaims, "Is there anything that would prevent me from being baptized right now? I'm ready, and I've been ready all my life."

What's remarkable about that story and the reason it's been preserved all these years is that no one expected a faith response from a person like this — a non-Jewish person. But there he was, giving expression to what all human beings feel inside: a hunger for God. And not the lesser gods of our lives, either, but the Creator of the universe, the God who first breathed life into us.

We were created on the sixth day — the same day as the animals. But what separates us from the animals is not our intelligence or our moral sense. What separates us is that we were created to be in relationship with God. We received God's image, God's likeness. We were created to reflect God's glory.

We were born for this, and until we see it, until we recognize what our lives were made for, until we wake up to God's never-ending pursuit of us, we are going to be hungry, restless, dissatisfied people, giving our allegiance to one or more of the lesser gods around us.

Let me ask you this: What are *you* using to fill the empty space inside you?

QUESTIONS FOR FURTHER STUDY AND REFLECTION

1. One of the people Jesus encountered during his ministry said, "I believe; help my unbelief." How does that describe your own faith?

2. Where are the places in your life right now where you have questions? How does your faith help you address them?

3. Make a mental list of the interests and activities that fill your life. Do you sense in one or more of them a deeper longing, a *spiritual* hunger?

Where We Find God

GENERAL REVELATION

The heavens are telling the glory of God;
   and the firmament proclaims his handiwork.
Day to day pours forth speech,
   and night to night declares knowledge.
There is no speech, nor are there words;
   their voice is not heard;
   yet their voice goes out through all the earth,
   and their words to the end of the world.

                    Psalm 19:1-4

HAVE YOU EVER sat in church on a Sunday morning, listening to the sermon or watching as a baby was baptized, and
thought to yourself, "How do they know that? How can they be
certain that that's all true?"

I read somewhere that whenever a preacher makes the claim
that God loves us or that God gives our brief lives meaning and
purpose, someone in the pews is saying silently but insistently,
"How does he know that?" or "How can she be so sure?"

Lots of people make religious claims, especially these days,
and so the question is a natural one.

How do we know?

Recently someone gave me a book about a church that, like
my own, is located in the Chicago suburbs. The pastor of that
church, according to the book, preached a sermon at his church's
founding in the early 1980s in which he said, "I stand before you
today confident that this dream [for a church] will become a reality. Why? Because this dream is inspired by God."

And I thought, "Aw, come on. How do you know that? What
makes you think it's not just your hungry soul wanting success?"
(To be fair about it, he does say later on in the book that he won-
ders about this same question from time to time. Is it really of
God?)

I think "How do you know?" is an important question, and
it deserves an answer. You and I should be able to give a thought-
ful answer. Maybe not to every cynic who asks the question. But
it seems to me we should be able to say how we know that what
we believe about God is true.

How do we know?

*   *   *

On a summer vacation not long ago, I went with my daughter
to see the recently released film *Contact*, which stars Jodi Foster.
The Jodi Foster character, who makes no claims to be a Christian —
at least not at the beginning of the film — is a scientist who devotes

16

her career to listening for signs of life from outer space by making use of enormous radio telescopes. At one point in the film, she asks, "If God created the universe, then why didn't he leave some fingerprints, some way of letting us know that he was here?" Those aren't the exact words, but that's the sense of her question. If God created the world, why don't we see some evidence of the divine hand in it? Now to me that's clearly a faith question, and you just don't hear questions like that very often in a major motion picture.

In a review of the movie I read, the late Gene Siskel wrote, "That one question makes the movie worth the price of admission." Well, given the price of admission today, I'm not quite sure about that, but he was right that the question is an important one. Ever since I heard it, I've been wanting to give the answer. I wanted to get up and speak right there in the theater. I figured somebody should say something. How do we know?

Christian faith and life are inseparable from reliable knowledge of the character and purpose of God. If we do not want to call the source of this knowledge revelation, then we will have to invent some other term to take its place.

Daniel L. Migliore, *Faith Seeking Understanding*

What Christian people believe is that we don't live in a silent or speechless world. To put that more positively, we believe in a God who speaks, who reveals himself, who in countless ways discloses himself to us. In fact, we believe that it is in God's very nature to want to be known — to want to be known *by us*. He has gone to extraordinary lengths to be known by us.

So, to put it plainly, we believe, first of all, that God reveals himself to us in creation. Psalm 19 says it best: "The heavens are telling the glory of God; and the firmament proclaims his handiwork." That's what we call "general revelation."

Next, we believe that God reveals himself to us in the relationship he has had with his people over the centuries. This is the biblical record, the story of God and his people, and we call it "special revelation," or the Bible, which I will describe in the next chapter.

And finally, we believe that God has revealed himself to us completely in the person of Jesus Christ. Everything we would want to know about God was present in Jesus Christ. That's the doctrine of the Incarnation, which we'll examine in the last chapter.

These are the ways we know about God. They all point us to God. But let's look first at general revelation.

* * *

Open, ye heavens, your living doors; let in
The great Creator from his work returned
Magnificent, his six days' work, a world.

John Milton, *Paradise Lost*

Theologians over the centuries have by no means been in agreement about the value of general revelation.

John Calvin is one theologian who was mostly enthusiastic about the value of general revelation. In one of his commentaries, he wrote that a child nursing at her mother's breast speaks to us more eloquently of the glory of God than a thousand oracles. Calvin went on to say that the universe was scattered with what he called sparks of glory. And when we see those sparks, we get a read, a fix on who God is.

It's the same way, I suppose, that we get to know an artist. We look at her paintings, and we come away with a better sense of who she is and what matters to her. We get a strong impression of her because the paintings, we believe, reveal or expose the artist to us.

But just as the artist is not her art, so of course God is not the same thing as creation; rather, creation is a magnificent reflection of the glory of God. By looking at creation, we can get a sense of who God is.

*   *   *

Not long ago, someone recommended a book to me by Michael Behe called *Darwin's Black Box*. It's not the sort of book I would have picked out on my own, but now that I've read it, I'm glad I did.

What Behe points out is that there's an intense debate in academic circles today about Charles Darwin and his theories. Quite a few scholars, it seems, have become militant and aggressive in the way they're promoting Darwin's theories — it's Darwinism with an attitude. Darwin, as you know, rejected God or the biblical account of creation as an explanation for how things came to be. Instead, he wrote about natural selection and randomness.

Behe, who makes no claims to be an evangelical Christian and is certainly not a supporter of the creationist theory, looks at the universe at the molecular level. He's a biochemist by training. And what he says is that Darwin is just plain wrong. Darwin's theories may explain many things, but at the molecular level they don't stand up.

In a chapter on blood clotting, which was very humbling for me to read because of its technical detail (college biology class is for me a distant memory), Behe says that the mechanisms of clotting are so complex — at a molecular level — and require such a precise interaction of complex parts that evolution couldn't possibly be an explanation for their existence. The odds against it, he says, are something like one-tenth to the eighteenth power, which is an extremely small number.

And the question is, Why? Well, he says, there wasn't time. Behe accepts a universe that's billions of years old, but even at that, he says, there wasn't enough time for something like blood clotting to have come into being.

19

It's so amazing, he says, that whenever you cut yourself and within minutes the wound begins to heal itself, the whole universe should stand up and clap its hands. At a molecular level it's an awe-inspiring event. Something as routine in our lives as blood clotting, he says, tells us that there is an intelligent design in the universe.

We may ignore, but we can nowhere evade,
    the presence of God.
The world is crowded with him.

C. S. Lewis, *Letters to Malcolm*

---

*   *   *

When we speak about general revelation, what we say is that it's available to all. That is its strength. It comes to all of us — the biochemist at Lehigh University and the Presbyterian in Wheaton. We can all see it, or at least catch glimpses of it.

But — and this is important to see — we also say that general revelation is dimmer than other kinds of revelation. By its very nature it is ambiguous and open to interpretation. You can always come away from it confused. Christians in South Africa looked at creation and thought they saw there a justification for their system of apartheid. They believed that God clearly intended the separation of the races. Other Christians, as we know, look at the evidence of creation and see something quite different.

One of the most important theologians of the twentieth century, Karl Barth, had very serious reservations about general revelation and warned Christians about the conclusions they drew from it. Creation, after all, is a mixed bag. Michael Behe says that blood clotting points to an intelligent designer, but you can't necessarily conclude from that that a loving and personal God, the God of the Christian, therefore exists. It's just not all that clear.

Or, you might have a great week, spiritually speaking, you might be very aware of God's presence in your life, and you might even venture to tell someone about it. But that person could very well look at the evidence and say to you, "That's not God, for Pete's sake. You've just had a few lucky days in a row. How do you get God out of that?"

Lesslie Newbigin, who spent most of his life as a missionary in India, says in one of his books that vast numbers of people in the world look at creation and come away thinking of God as terribly impersonal, as the great unknown, as someone who doesn't really care about you and me.

* * *

So, general revelation is always going to be incomplete by itself, and what's required to see it more clearly, many Christians believe, is at least a modest amount of faith.

Elizabeth Achtemeier, a theologian in the Reformed tradition, uses the image of highway reflectors when she writes about general revelation. By themselves, highway reflectors don't do very much, but when you shine your headlights in their direction, it's as though they come alive. It's at that point that they begin to do their job.

Similarly, Achtemeier writes, unless we come to the world in the skin of Jesus Christ, in faith, we're going to miss the signs that are out there. General revelation always needs to be grounded in something more.

* * *

Here's something else I think we should know about general revelation. It has what theologians like to call objective and subjective sides. I've already described revelation's objective side, which is the information or the data we get from the world around us.

But it's important not to miss the subjective side. Christians believe that revelation always calls forth a response.

Because we've been created with a sense of the divine, what Calvin called the *sensus divinitatus* — because we have this capacity to recognize God, we are able to respond.

One of our responsibilities as people of faith, I believe, is to nurture this capacity so that we can respond fully and appreciatively. So often, you see, we remove ourselves from places where we *can* catch glimpses of God. We often live our lives in such a way that the occasions for seeing God are limited. It's as though we're all living in the city, and the lights of the city are making it hard for us to see the stars. And so it's only when we're out in the country or when we're at that special place by the lake that we look up and say, "Oh my, will you look at that! I had no idea. Isn't that something!"

So many of us are waking up in the morning to "The Today Show" and going to bed at night with "The Tonight Show" that we don't allow ourselves to hear the still, small voice of God. Our lives are crowded with background noise morning, noon, and night. And in it all God's voice gets lost. How can we hear, much less respond, if we don't train ourselves to listen, if we don't make time to listen for God in our lives, if we don't allow ourselves to be open to God's presence?

We seek evidence of God in the natural world. . . . But we must not forget to look for him in the depths of our soul.

François de Fénelon,
Meditations and Devotions

I have a friend who recently spent a year studying art at a school on the East Coast. She's a gifted artist herself, and the year there was a tribute to her gifts. When she came home, I said, "How was it?" And she said, "Oh, I think I'm so much better at observing the world around me." Naturally I asked her what she meant by that, but later I thought, "She's right. To grow is to open ourselves and to become receptive. We all need to train ourselves to become better observers, better listeners."

How could that not be true in terms of faith as well?

*　　*　　*

Here's a dimension to revelation that some people have probably never considered: when God reveals himself to us, it's often in the stuff of the earth. This is true of the written record, the Bible, which is a collection of books written by some very human authors. This is true of Jesus himself, who, although he was divine, was also very human — in some ways *disturbingly* human, as we will see in a later chapter. When God communicates with us, it's often in ways that we can see, touch, and hear.

The Bible makes this very clear: no one has ever seen God. We always see or hear God indirectly. Even in John's Gospel when Jesus says, "If you have seen me, you have seen the Father," the sense you get is that the disciples aren't really seeing the fullness of God's glory.

In the Old Testament book of Exodus, chapter 33, Moses and God have a conversation. They're friends, and it's a wonderful story of closeness and intimacy. At one point, Moses says to God, "Show me your face. I want to see what you look like."

And God, as we might expect, says, "You can't see my face because no one can see my face and live."

As we listen in on this conversation, we might say, "Moses, what are you thinking about? You don't know what you're asking!"

But God says, "Here's what I'll do. I'll put you in the cleft of the rock, and then I'll pass by." And as God passes by, it is God — not Moses — who shields Moses' eyes. God reaches out, in such a tender gesture, and covers Moses' eyes until he has passed by, and then Moses is allowed to see God's back, perhaps a metaphor for this indirect way of seeing.

What does that story mean? I think it can mean this: we see

23

evidence of where God goes, but usually not until after he's gone. We see evidence in the birth of children, let's say, or we see it in a relationship that endures the test of time and distance. We don't see God's feet, but we see his footprints. We don't see God's hands, but we see his fingerprints.

I say, "Here we are in the wonderful presence of the One who loves us." And if someone asks me, "How do you know?" I answer, "Well, God has revealed himself in creation, then in the Scriptures, and finally in Jesus Christ. More than that, my own mom and dad told me about him. I've listened to the saints, who have lived in faith before me. And if that's not enough, there is this conviction in me that is so strong, a conviction born of the Spirit of God."

That's how I know. How do *you* know?

QUESTIONS FOR FURTHER STUDY AND REFLECTION

1. Where in the universe — or in your own life — do you find evidence for the existence of God? If you pointed out this evidence to other people, what would *they* see?

2. Why should Christians be careful or cautious with general revelation? Can you think of specific examples where Christians have misinterpreted or misread the "evidence" of nature?

3. Read Romans 1:16-25 and Acts 17:23. What does the Apostle Paul say about a natural knowledge of God?

What the Bible Is

SPECIAL REVELATION

All scripture is inspired by God and is useful for teaching, for reproof, for correction, and for training in righteousness, so that everyone who belongs to God may be proficient, equipped for every good work.

2 Timothy 3:16-17

PEOPLE WHO CALL themselves Christians believe that God speaks to them through the words of the Bible. Which, when you think about it, is quite a claim, isn't it?

God speaks to us.

On the one hand, it's a wonderful truth, a reason for celebration. It might be the reason you're taking the time to read this chapter right now — in the hope that it might be true. On the other hand, it's preposterous, isn't it? The claim that God speaks to us today through a collection of books written many centuries ago? Who could believe such a thing?

In this chapter I intend to reflect on what this claim might mean.

God speaks to us.

*   *   *

In his book called *Rumor of Angels,* Lutheran thinker and sociologist Peter Berger makes a helpful comparison between a Christian and a cultural anthropologist doing fieldwork.

As Berger describes it, the cultural anthropologist out in the field is always in danger of forgetting what her true identity is. And so, Berger says, there is always the risk that she will "go native." That's his phrase.

Unless the cultural anthropologist makes frequent trips home or links herself with others like her on the field, more than likely she *will* go native. Very quickly, in spite of herself, she'll adopt the ways and the customs of the people she is attempting to study.

That's the way it is, Berger argues, for people who call themselves Christians. There is always this danger, this risk, of going native, of being absorbed by the culture around us. We have a tendency to forget who we are and what our true identity is.

Paul's letter to Timothy (especially 2 Timothy 3) has often been cited by Christian people over the years as a helpful way to understand the Bible and how we are to use it. Whenever I read

Paul's words, I find it helpful to think of Berger's comparison between the Christian and the cultural anthropologist because in his letter Paul too talks about the danger of going native.

Paul describes the culture in which Timothy lives as self-indulgent. The people are lovers of self, money, and pleasure. In fact, Paul writes a long litany of behaviors he notices in the surrounding culture, and the description isn't flattering. The first few verses of chapter three offer an interesting glimpse into the first-century world. Paul describes a culture that has turned in on itself.

And then Paul says to Timothy, his young protégé, "Be careful out there. Don't go native. Remember who you are and what you were taught. Remember what your true identity is."

It's in that context that Paul mentions Scripture. He says, "Remember what you were taught, how from an early age you were schooled in the scriptures. Those are the words that will make you strong."

[The Bible] is the story of the one God,
    who is the Father, the Son, and the Holy Spirit.
That story is still unfolding,
    and in faith we make it our own.
It forms our memory and our hope.
It tells us who we are and what we are to do.
To retell it is to declare what we believe.

A Declaration of Faith, 1985 (PCUSA)

Like cultural anthropologists, Christian people also need to make regular contact with home. We have been given an identity in our baptisms that sets us apart from the culture in which we find ourselves. In baptism we were all adopted as God's sons and daughters. That's who we are. But we find ourselves in the field, so to speak, and we face the constant danger that we too will go native, that we'll forget who we are.

It has occurred to me, as I have reflected on this, that the comparison between us and cultural anthropologists is really going to make sense only if we recognize how foreign the culture in which we live really is.

I don't know about you, but I am reminded almost daily that I am out of step with the world around me. All I have to do is watch a television sitcom with my teenage daughter to remember that I'm different. My values are not the values of my neighbors (though there are some wonderful exceptions). The vocation — or the calling — that I have felt to give my life in service to others is certainly not the vocation that I hear my neighbors describe. I live here and work here, in this culture, but this is not my home. This culture feels strange to me.

Our home, as the Apostle Paul puts it to Timothy, is described in the words of Scripture. The Bible is where we learn about and are reminded of our true identity.

We are "people of the Book." You've heard that expression, I'm sure, and what it means is that the Bible is our reference point. In a churning sea of opinions and theories and beliefs, which describes our culture today, there is one constant, one source of authority.

And we are glad to obey. Or are we?

*   *   *

As I write this, I realize just how countercultural this belief really is. When Christians — or people of faith — claim that there is an authority in our lives, and that it's the Bible, we are swimming against the current of culture.

Ever since the Enlightenment, there has been a powerful movement away from fixed truths and certainties. "No pope and no king" is the legacy we've inherited. "No pope and no king will tell me what to do and what to believe. No church and no government will direct my life." That's the historical legacy that I have inherited as a Presbyterian. But one source of authority that we have clung to is the Bible. And it's odd, in a way — this reverence

Jesus Christ, as he is attested for us in Holy Scripture, is
the one Word of God which we have to hear and which
we have to trust and obey in life and in death.

The Theological Declaration of Barmen, 1934

for a set of old books. In case you haven't noticed, it's not at all
what people around us think or believe.

Psalm 119 is a tribute to, a celebration of God's law, God's
word. Psalm 119 is the longest psalm in the book, and scholars
point out that in its Hebrew form it's something like an acrostic
puzzle — with every stanza or section starting with a different letter of the Hebrew alphabet. Psalm 119 says, among other things,
that God's law is "sweeter than honey." It's a "lamp to our feet"
and a "light to our path."

Well, that's just odd, isn't it? Let me tell you, if you believe
that, you're out of step with the world around you.

*   *   *

Peter Gomes, who is the pastor of the Memorial Church at Harvard University, which makes him a religious leader on that cam-
pus, has written a very interesting book. It's called *The Good Book*.
As you might expect, it's all about the Bible.

Gomes cites the usual statistics about the biblical ignorance
that affects Christians today. For example, 10 percent of those
surveyed think that Joan of Arc was Noah's wife. Sixteen percent
are convinced that the New Testament contains a gospel by the
Apostle Thomas. And 28 percent — almost a third of those surveyed — believe that both the Old *and* the New Testaments were
written just a few years after Jesus' death. Gomes writes that it reminds him of an old Sunday school joke:

Q. What are the epistles?
A. They're the wives of the apostles.

And then he goes on to make an observation that I think is right on target: What's astounding about this — the woeful ignorance of most people when it comes to the Bible — is that most Christian people would describe the Bible as the most important source of authority in their lives. They would describe the Bible as their home, the one place they can turn to in order to remember who they are and what their true identity is.

In a way, of course, it's not surprising. Given the culture in which we live, given the legacy of the Enlightenment that questions all authority, it's not surprising that even people of faith would begin to go native, to lose touch with home. It's not surprising that even Christians would begin to say, "How do you know? How do you know that God speaks to us in these words? And if you don't know for sure, then why spend a lot of time reading them?"

Here are two ways we know that God speaks to us in the words of Scripture. These are important insights that the church has long claimed, and I think people of faith should be familiar with them. We should know at least this much about the good book.

1. *The Bible is self-authenticating.* That's a good phrase to remember, and let me give you an example of what it means.

If someone were asking me about the value of love or friendship, if someone wanted to know how I could value something like love or friendship for myself, I'd probably start by describing what love is or what friendship looks like. I might get a book off the shelf in my study and point out what other people, the great writers, have said about love or friendship.

But then, if the person who was asking me persisted, if that person wanted to know how I as a reasonable person could believe in something like love or friendship, I think I would say, "Get out and mingle! Meet some people and see for yourself. Get to know them and discover what friendship might feel like. If you want to know what love is, date someone, for heaven's sake. And maybe you'll experience the feeling that I've come to know."

When Christian people say that the truths of the Bible are self-authenticating, what we're really saying is, "See for yourself. If you want to know if you can trust it, put yourself in there. And you will find, as we have, that God's promises are reliable and trustworthy."

I look at the promises that God made to Abraham and Sarah way back in the Old Testament — for example, "In you all the nations of the world will be blessed" — and then I look at Western Christians today. And what I see is that we are just basking, *basking*, in the promises of God. Has God kept his promises to you? I would say that he has, and the church has said — from the beginning it has said — "See, God can be trusted to do what he said he would do." The words of Scripture authenticate themselves.

The Spirit breathes upon the Word,
And brings the truth to sight;
Precepts and promises afford
A sanctifying light.

William Cowper, *Hymn*

---

2. The other insight that the church has passed along regarding Scripture goes something like this: *We need to read the words of Scripture with assistance.* By ourselves we're going to be lost.

I mentioned this belief in a sermon not long ago, and afterward someone made a point of finding me and asking, "Does that mean you're opposed to personal devotions?" And I answered, "No, of course not." But when we read the Bible, even if we read by ourselves, we need to think of ourselves as surrounded by the community of the faithful. It's *as though* we read the Bible together.

People of faith believe that the primary function of the Bible is its use in worship, and then of course we really do read the Bi-

31

ble together. It's in the reading of the Bible, the proclamation, and the sacraments, we say, that Christ himself becomes real to us. Much more could be said about this, but for now I just want to note that individual study of the Bible is really only a derivative of its primary function, which is its use in worship.

I have a dear friend who recently, in a time of crisis, decided to sit down and read the whole Bible, from beginning to end. When he was finished, he said to me, "Now I understand." Not having reached that point myself, I was somewhat skeptical, and so I asked, "What do you mean?" He began to tell me the results of his research — which is how he thought of his reading — and I was shaken by what he said, because his conclusions were so far from what we would call traditional orthodoxy.

It's dangerous to go to Scripture alone. It's why preachers who prepare sermons spend time reading the commentaries. It's important to know what others have said. It's important that our own views be shaped and molded by the faithful who have gone before us. And not only that, but it's arrogant to think that we as individuals can come to Scripture and just make up our own minds about what it means.

But it's not just the commentaries that help us to understand and hear God's word to us. It's also the Spirit of God. John Calvin, the reformer in whose tradition I stand, once wrote that we need the spectacles of faith when we read the words of the Bible. That's a helpful image for me. For the words of Scripture to become God's word to us, the Holy Spirit must move in us, and then — and only then — are we able to see.

In his book *The Trivialization of God*, Presbyterian minister Donald McCullough writes that the church didn't first invent the theory of divine inspiration and then, on that basis, confer authority on the sixty-six books that make up our Bible. Not at all. Those sixty-six books formed themselves, is how he puts it. They asserted their own authority. As people of faith read them, it slowly became clear that here were the words of God to us. Not in other books written at the same time, but in these books.

People often have this idea that the Bible came together

suddenly, and the truth is, it was a slow process. It was painful at times. And the church is still not of one mind about what belongs and what doesn't. The Protestant Bible, for example, looks different from the Catholic Bible. If you've come to the Protestant church from the Catholic church, you've probably noticed that. And the reason is that the Bible took a long time to come together. Slowly, over time — over centuries, in fact — the faithful have agreed on what belongs there and what does not.

O Lord, heavenly Father, in whom is the fullness of light and wisdom, enlighten our minds by your Holy Spirit, and give us grace to receive your Word with reverence and humility, without which no one can understand your truth. For Christ's sake, Amen.

John Calvin, "Before Reading Scripture"

Occasionally church members will say to me, "I've been reading the Bible, and I just don't get certain things" or "I'm troubled by what I'm finding there." And it's true that there are difficult passages: the drowning of people with a flood, the command by God that Abraham sacrifice his son Isaac, and more. It's possible to come away from the Bible shaking your head — and more than that: it's possible to come away wanting to reject its authority altogether.

Which would be a shame.

Not long ago I heard a story that seemed to offer a helpful way of thinking about the Bible. We hear, don't we, that chicken, properly prepared and processed, is a good food for us to eat? And when we hear that, we seem to know, don't we, that there are certain parts of the chicken that are better for us than others? The feathers, the bones, the cartilage — these are parts we wouldn't think of trying to eat.

I would say that the Bible is like that. To someone who is

33

struggling to understand, I would say, "Stay with the familiar for now. Go with what feels comfortable. It's hard to go wrong with the Gospels, for example — Matthew, Mark, Luke, and John. Study them and become familiar with them. And then later, as you feel more comfortable, as you become more conversant with the world in which the Bible was written, maybe you'll be able to go further. Maybe you won't choke on the bones."

*   *   *

One last thing. It is important to remember that the Bible points us to Jesus Christ, that the Bible is a witness to the living Word. I want to end this chapter by saying briefly what that means.

The Bible contains many different kinds of writing — history, geography, and even a smattering of science. And while some of that may be interesting, what's most important, what's most reliable, is what the Bible says about Jesus Christ. That's what our confessions are trying to tell us. When the Bible points us to Jesus Christ, it's at that point that we need to sit up and take notice.

When you start to read the Bible for what it says about history and geography and science, there's always a danger of misreading the message. For several months there was a book on the *New York Times* best-seller list called *The Bible Code,* written by Michael Drosnin. Contrary to what that author believes, the Bible was never intended to let us know mysteriously or cryptically the exact timing of world events. That sort of interpretation might make for an interesting book or an entertaining movie, but that's not what the Bible is about.

The Bible points us to Jesus Christ and demonstrates in countless ways how we can be more and more like him. Jesus Christ is always the goal and destination of the Christian life. If we're not heading that way, then we need to stop and get directions.

What I've been saying in this chapter is that the Bible is the place where we stop to get those directions. Admittedly, the Bible can be a tough book to read, and it's difficult sometimes to enter into it. The Bible makes us work. But for me the challenge is always this: How can I know better the God who loves me and who loved countless people before me? How can I know better this person Jesus Christ, who was sent to be God with us? How can I find my way home?

The next time you read the Bible, read it with that in mind.

QUESTIONS FOR FURTHER STUDY AND REFLECTION

1. People make many different claims for the Bible and what it tells us. Can you say, specifically, what the Bible tells us *about* God?

2. In what sense do Christians believe that the Bible is the "Word of God"?

3. Is the Bible the authority — or even *an* authority — in your life?

Who God Is

THE FIRST PERSON OF THE TRINITY

God is not something but someone, not just a "spiritual force" but a person. Biblical-Christian faith is faith in a *personal* God.

Shirley C. Guthrie, *Christian Doctrine*

WHEN YOU SAY the word "God" or, better yet, when you think about God, what image comes to your mind? What I'm really asking, I suppose, is what lies behind that word for you. What is the *content* of that word for you?

Robert Coles, who for many years taught psychiatry at Harvard University, had a special interest in children, and toward the end of his teaching career — which included many books — he wrote a book called *The Spiritual Life of Children*. For his research, Coles found children all over the world, in many different cultures, and he spoke with them about their understanding of God. It's a fascinating book, full of pictures that children drew for him and stories that children told — an amazing collection of information and insight.

One of the insights that Coles comes away with is that all or just about all children, apparently, have a sense of God — no matter where they grow up, no matter what the circumstances of their lives. This sense of God is nearly universal. Which is something I mentioned in the introduction of this book.

Beyond that, Coles found — and maybe this isn't terribly surprising — that the sense of God which we seem to start out with in life is then shaped and molded by the culture in which we live, by our circumstances. If you grow up in abject poverty, for example, your understanding of God will be shaped by that. If you grow up with loving and emotionally available parents, your understanding of God will be shaped by that. And so on. The variables of our lives play a huge role in the way we think about God.

Now, as I said, this may not be terribly surprising, but when I read it, I started to wonder about the Christian people I know and their images of God. How much have our environment, our culture, and our privileged communities shaped the way we understand who God is?

And more than that, if we could peel some of that away, if we could get rid of the odd notions that we've attached to God along the way (the ones that may say more about who we are than they do about who God is), if we could somehow get back to that childhood sense that we all started out with, then what? Would we be surprised by what we had left? Would we be moved or touched in any way? Would we fall to our knees in wonder and awe and thanksgiving?

One of the drawings that Coles includes in his book is one he calls "the planet where God lives." As the child who made this drawing imagines it, God lives on a planet that is visible in the night sky, and the planet is beautiful, colorful, and alive. But the planet is also out there. And in the picture the child is standing here, on earth, looking up to the sky, where he sees this wonderful planet. What's wrenching about this picture, Coles says, is that, although the child has a smile on his face, the planet is out of his reach. It's distant. God exists for him — no doubt about that — but God is also not a part of his life.

I had approached God, or my idea of God, without love, without awe, even without fear. He was . . . to appear neither as Savior nor as Judge, but merely as a magician.

C. S. Lewis, describing his childhood conception of God in *Surprised by Joy*

What that child seems to grasp intuitively is where many people seem to have ended up. This century, as you probably know, has come to be known as the "Death of God" era. It was the German philosopher Friedrich Nietzsche who first proposed the idea, and in the 1960s, especially, it was debated passionately — at least in academic circles. And at one point the question "Is God dead?" even appeared on the cover of *Time* magazine.

Coming on the heels of World War II, the second major war of the century, and the murder of some six million Jews, who, after all, were God's chosen people, the concept was hard to dismiss. Some very serious Jewish thinkers (and even some non-

Jewish thinkers) argue that it's no longer possible to believe in God. They say that the monstrous events of our century prove that if there ever was a powerful, just, compassionate God, that God is now dead.

For some people this is a frightening issue to contemplate, but as I think about it, maybe there's something about it that's not all bad. Maybe it was time — not for God to die, of course, but for a particular way of thinking about God to die. Maybe it was time for some tired old ideas to pass away. Maybe the God who ought to die is the God who is nothing more than a heavenly grandfather, benignly smiling and doting on all of us, his beloved grandchildren. Maybe that idea no longer fits with the evidence of our world, if it ever did.

Or how about the God who finds us parking places when we need them, or the God who makes our lives safe and comfortable and warm? The God who asks nothing from us and gives us everything we want? The God who automatically forgives everything anytime, no matter how awful our behavior? Maybe it's time for that God to die as well.

The God who is called the Supreme Being, the Almighty — you know the One, invoked by countless politicians over the decades — maybe it's time that God died too. He never did do much of anything, except bless whatever we in this country wanted to do in his name. Maybe it's time he died. No one is going to miss him much anyway.

What I want to do in this chapter is to reintroduce God to us, the God of the Bible. What I want to do is to peel away as many layers as I can that we have attached over the years. This God, I believe, is far different from the God I see acknowledged and talked about today.

*   *   *

Who is God for us?

When you read the Bible — slowly, thoughtfully, and carefully — you don't read much, if any, speculation about who God is. The Bible doesn't make many pronouncements about God. There isn't much philosophical talk about God and hardly any debatable propositions about him, either. Instead, what the Bible does most of the time is tell us about a God in action, a God in motion. The God we meet in the Bible acts, speaks, knows, wills, decides, loves, rejoices, regrets, pleads, judges, changes his mind at the last minute, rules, triumphs, and suffers pain. The God we meet in the Bible can be angry, compassionate, jealous, and merciful — and sometimes God can be all of those things in the course of just a few verses.

And so the sense you get when you read the biblical record is not that God is a spiritual force or power in the world; the sense you get is that God is a person. God is personal first of all. And then God talks — not to himself, but to us. So God also desires relationship. God is intensely invested in his creation, takes pride in it, and of course feels sorrow too — especially when creation is marred and abused.

The God we believe in is accessible — at least in the sense that he wants to be known by us. God has gone out of his way to reveal himself to us in ways that we, his creatures, can comprehend and understand.

Over the centuries, theologians have called this dimension of God *immanence*. In a way, you see, it's one of the most surprising and pleasing of God's characteristics. We can know God, and furthermore, he wants to be known by us.

But there is a downside to all of this, too. The God who is near and available and desires relationship with us can also be a

---

The imagination enlarges little objects so as to fill our soul with its fantastic estimate, and by a rash insolence belittles the great to its own measure, as when it speaks of God.

Blaise Pascal, *Pensées*

God who is not feared, a God who isn't taken seriously, a God who expects little and demands nothing.

One recent summer, when the high-school youth from my church went to a conference in Florida, they met an actor named Curt Clonninger during one of the evening meetings. He's become known for his powerful portrayals of God. What he presents are caricatures of the distorted images we have of God. He's got a whole series of them, and they're very entertaining even as they make their point. At the conference, he would do one of his portrayals on stage, and then the audience would divide up into small groups and talk about it.

What was fascinating to me, and reassuring too, was that our young people could see the sort of God that has been introduced to them in their own community — and furthermore, they could see that they really wanted no part of this God.

The "party animal" was the portrayal that the young people from my church seemed to pick out as the dominant image of God in their community. That was the name Clonninger gave to this particular character. This "party animal" God calls everybody "Sugar" and does it in the most endearing way. This "party animal" God winks at our foibles and weaknesses, accepts anything we do as charming, makes no demands on us, and just wants us to have a good time — whatever that may be for us.

And guess what? The kids from my church know that just isn't so. They've been introduced to a "party animal" God in our culture that's a counterfeit, a phony. The God they see worshipped and talked about in our culture isn't worth their time. He isn't worth ours, either. And they know it.

So it has occurred to me that maybe what Christian people really need to remember is that God has still another dimension or side. There is the *immanent* side to God, as we've seen, but theologians also speak of a *transcendent* side to God. And as you know, when we speak of God's transcendence, it's then that we speak about God as eternal, omniscient, omnipresent, immutable, infinite, and incomprehensible. These are some of the traditional ways to refer to God's transcendence.

THE FIRST PERSON OF THE TRINITY

It's in the presence of this God that words fail us. We fall silent, and we worship. The prophet Isaiah, in chapter 55, has this God saying, "My thoughts are not your thoughts, nor are my ways your ways." Let's get that straight, God seems to be saying.

Earlier in Isaiah's prophecy, in chapter 6, we read about Isaiah's encounter with God in the temple, and we read there that the foundations of the temple shake with God's presence. The room fills with smoke, and hideous, multi-winged creatures fly about. This is what theologians and poets alike have called the *mysterium tremendum*. There is in the Bible this clear message that God is different from us, Wholly Other, and in some ways even frightening, awful. In Exodus 33:20, for example, we read the statement that God makes to Moses: "No one can see me and live."

I think we've lost some of that. Christian people today have lost an appreciation for the transcendent side of God. In our headlong rush to make God seem approachable and comfortable and easygoing, we've toned down, tamed, and domesticated God. In the process we have let go of something terribly important.

Can you find out the deep things of God?
Can you find out the limit of the Almighty?
It is higher than heaven.

Job 11:7-8

---

*　　*　　*

I have known people who decided to read the Bible on their own, and they've said to me, "Oh, I don't think I ever saw it before, but, you know, God changes. From Old Testament to New Testament, God undergoes a change." One friend put it to me this way: "God realized that the old style of fear and intimidation didn't work anymore, so in the New Testament he's kinder and gentler." On the surface maybe it does look as though the God who thunders on Mount Sinai gives way to the New Testament God we meet in Jesus.

But look deeper. The truth of the matter is that God reveals himself to us always with these two sides or dimensions. Isaiah tells us about a mysterious and powerful God in one breath, but then he also speaks compellingly of God as a mother who comforts her children. Martin Luther seemed to say that the two sides or dimensions of God are contradictory. John Calvin, whose career as a reformer of the Roman Catholic Church overlapped that of Luther, in effect said, "No, the two sides are complementary. Only when they're taken together do we fully understand who God is."

C. S. Lewis, in his book *The Lion, the Witch, and the Wardrobe,* wrestles with this same issue and does it at a level that children can understand. Every book in the Chronicles of Narnia series is, in a sense, a little theological textbook.

In *The Lion, the Witch, and the Wardrobe,* there is a scene where Mr. and Mrs. Beaver are having a conversation with Lucy about Aslan, the lion, who obviously represents God. And Lucy asks, "Is he safe?" And Mr. Beaver answers, "Safe . . . who said anything about safe? 'Course he isn't safe. But he's good. He's the King, I tell you."

*   *   *

How, exactly, does a person talk about God?

Sometimes the Bible uses masculine terms such as "father," "king," "husband," and "warrior." Occasionally, though admittedly not as often, the Bible uses feminine terms to describe God, and in those cases God is like a wife, a mother giving birth, a mother protecting her young, and even a mother comforting a frightened child. The truth is, all of our language about God is going to be limited, imprecise, and even crude. Our language about God is going to be anthropomorphic — in other words, ascribing human characteristics to a being who is most certainly not human.

Is it accurate to describe God exclusively in male terms? Or, for that matter, exclusively in female terms? No, God has no gender. Neither male nor female terms can ever adequately describe who God is. Most pastors I know struggle mightily to use language about God that is accurate, reverent, and not jarring. In my preaching I attempt to model what I believe about God, but more work still needs to be done in this area — perhaps by poets and theologians together.

So how can we speak about God? Maybe the best answer is simply this: We need to be aware that our language about God will always be an approximation. God will never be limited to the words we use to describe him.

*   *   *

Now, some people are going to hear all of this and say, "Well, why does it have to be so complicated? Why can't there be a simpler explanation for who God is? We're always taking things and making them far more complicated than they really have to be. I prefer a simple faith. 'Jesus loves me, this I know, for the Bible tells me so.'"

And to this all I can say is, Look at the evidence. What I've described in this chapter is how God reveals himself to us. It's anything but simple. Just wait until we talk about the Trinity. That's not a simple concept, either, but it's a way to make sense of the evidence we see. To borrow the words of C. S. Lewis, "God isn't safe, but he's good." And somehow, mysteriously, those two ideas must fit together.

*   *   *

Early on in biblical history, God revealed his name to Moses, and from that time forward God's name was treated with a special reverence. In fact, no one spoke it out loud. And even today no one is quite sure how it should be pronounced. Whenever God's name appears in the Hebrew scriptures, Orthodox Jewish readers and even most Conservative Jewish readers will, out of reverence, not say the name, and instead substitute "the Lord."

God said to Moses, "I AM WHO I AM." He said further, "Thus you shall say to the Israelites, 'I AM has sent me to you.'"

Exodus 3:14

I first became aware of this practice when I studied Hebrew at Princeton Theological Seminary. Some undergraduate students — Jewish students — from the university would come over to take Hebrew classes, and out of deference to them we took up this practice of not saying God's name aloud, of substituting "the Lord" whenever it appeared. Over the years that small, seemingly inconsequential act of reverence has had an effect on me.

At the time, as I reflect on it now, there weren't many places in my life where I showed any reverence at all. But slowly I became aware that there was this God who not only loved me but who demanded something from me. This God whose name we so lightly use is the creator of the universe, of all things seen and unseen. This God whose presence we often take for granted — whose face is brighter than a thousand exploding suns — this God wants something from you and from me. And this God won't rest until he gets it.

If, suddenly, you found yourself in his presence, you would be different, wouldn't you? If you lived with the awareness that this God was right here with you, you would live and act differently, wouldn't you?

Well, the truth is, for people who call themselves Christian, God *is* here. What do you say about that?

QUESTIONS FOR FURTHER STUDY AND REFLECTION

1. "God is not something but someone," writes theologian Shirley Guthrie. Explain what this means to you and your faith.

2. Human language about God is always going to be limited. Can you think of specific instances where the language you heard or read about God was especially limited? What words didn't feel quite right? And why?

3. Life experiences sometimes distort or affect our understanding of God. Can you name one or more of the experiences in your own life that distorts or affects *your* understanding of God?

What God Does

PART ONE: CREATION

Q. *What do you believe when you say, "I believe in God,*
   the Father almighty, creator of heaven and earth"?
A. That the eternal Father of our Lord Jesus Christ,
      who out of nothing created heaven and earth
         and everything in them,
      who still upholds and rules them
         by his eternal counsel and providence,
      is my God and Father
         because of Christ his Son.

   Lord's Day 9, Heidelberg Catechism, 1563

ONE SUMMER not long ago a small dune buggy rolled slowly over the surface of the planet Mars, took some remarkable pictures, and then transmitted them many, many miles back to earth. What impressed me most about those pictures was that they showed how beautiful *earth* is.

Mars seems like such a cold, barren, and inhospitable place. My own backyard, by way of contrast, is awash in color and teeming with life, plant *and* animal. The most recent Mars landing was a reminder for me of the beauty of God's creation: the severe beauty of the planet Mars and the more familiar beauty here on our own planet.

Annie Dillard, in her book *Pilgrim at Tinker Creek,* has a chapter titled "Seeing." One of the stories she tells there is about a young woman, twenty-two years old, who was blind. She had surgery to restore her sight, and then later had her bandages removed. But when the bandages first came off, apparently the light was too bright, so the young woman immediately shut her eyes and wouldn't open them again for another two weeks. When she finally did, Dillard says, the young woman kept mumbling over and over again, "O God, how beautiful. O God, how beautiful."

Later in the book, Dillard writes that when people of faith die, they ought to respond as though they are leaving a wonderful dinner party. And to the host at the door, they should say over and over again, "Thank you. Thank you." The words "thank you," she writes, ought to be the last words on believers' lips as they pass from this life to the next.

Whenever Christian people worship, we come to say thank you to the God who made it all. God created the heavens and the earth, and we gather in worship for the purpose of remembering that — remembering that God is the creator of all that is, talking together about what it means, and then discovering the implications of it for our lives. And there are many.

*   *   *

So much could be said. So much in the history of theology has been rolled up in this one doctrine. In fact, I can't emphasize enough the importance of the doctrine of creation in the history of theology. Sometimes Christian ethics or Christian political philosophy will have their beginning in the doctrine of creation because theologians over the centuries have noticed what seems to them to be a clear pattern or structure to God's creation, and from this pattern or structure theologians will then draw conclusions about God's intentions for us and the way we ought to live.

*   *   *

Let me make just a few observations in this chapter.

The first two or three chapters of Genesis have been as hotly debated over the years as any chapters of the Bible. And rightly so. Those chapters are packed with meaning, though Christians are hardly in agreement about how those chapters should be interpreted.

> God of the sky,
> God of the sea,
> God of the rock
> and bird and tree,
> you are also
> the God of me.
>
> Luci Shaw, "Small Song"

Some Christians like to say that the creation account we find in Genesis was never intended to be a *scientific* description of how the universe came to be. It's more of a poem, they say, than a journalistic description of what happened. And yet, most biblical scholars agree that the description of creation in Genesis is, at least in part, a scientific account, reflecting the prevailing world-view or cosmology of the writers, often described by Old Testament scholars as the "priestly writers." They were writing the best science of their day.

There are some Christians today who take a very different approach. They like to read the creation story in a very literal way. And for them a literal reading means that the text is historically accurate and scientifically reliable. In other words, they say that to accept the authority and accuracy of the Bible, you have to dismiss many of the assumptions of modern science. The scientific assumption, for example, that the universe is billions of years old would have to be abandoned because it appears to contradict the biblical record contained in the first chapter of Genesis.

My own sense is that both of these interpretations are seriously flawed. The first interpretation underestimates the intent of the original writers, and the second often puts Christian people in an awkward and unnecessary battle with modern science. Is there another way to read this account? I think there is.

The goal of the biblical writers, I believe, was to tell us *why* we are here, not *how* we got here. The Bible, as I mentioned in the chapter on special revelation, is not first of all a science textbook. The Bible is always going to be most helpful to us when it lets us know who God is and what God is doing. Another way to read the Bible literally — and the creation story in particular — is to accept what has been called "the plain sense of the text."

In the plainest sense of all, the creation account in Genesis is a *proclamation*. The creation story is intended to teach and to proclaim the good news. God speaks volumes to us in these verses about who he is (and therefore who we are). As a matter of fact, we believe that is the single most important truth contained in the doctrine of creation: God created. That's the starting point in life for any person of faith. That's the singular truth with which we begin any conversation, any inquiry about the human condition, almost any thinking at all.

God created.

Many scholars believe that the first chapters of Genesis were written, or at least reached their final form, during the Babylo-

I asked the whole frame of the world about my God;
and it answered me, "I am not He, but He made me."

Augustine, *Confessions*

nian exile. After God's people had been conquered by a foreign army and dragged off to live in a strange land, their story was written down. They wanted to rediscover their identity. It was a time, as you can imagine, when they had little hope, and so the message of these verses is, "God created the heavens and the earth, and our God will not forsake what he himself has created." That was good news.

But that's not all. These words are also polemical, argumentative. They're fighting words. To the Persians, another ancient people, who worshipped the light, the creation story says, "No, God is the creator of light." To the Babylonians, who worshipped the sun, the moon, and the stars, the creation story says, "No, they are the servants of God — they exist at God's beck and call." To the Canaanites, who made sex and fertility their gods, it says, "No, God created our sexuality and fertility. Sexuality and fertility aren't gods; they may be gifts, but they're not gods." To our own culture today, which worships the self and whatever the self happens to want, the creation story says, "No, God is the creator, and we are the creatures. We don't live for ourselves; we live only to reflect God's glory."

One of the heresies that the church has struggled with over the years is *pantheism*, which says that God is in everything or, better yet, that everything is God. To that point of view the doctrine of creation says, "No, there's a difference between the Creator and what he has made."

Similarly, there's a new teaching being discussed in a variety of circles today, and to some it has a New Age feeling. It's called *panentheism,* and its proponents say, basically, that creation is an extension of God — like the mind is an extension of the body. All of creation is in God, and God surrounds creation.

I think I can understand why a teaching like panentheism has emerged. There's something attractive about it, because it seems to answer critical questions about the nature of God, but most Christian thinkers today believe that panentheism doesn't adequately explain the mystery of God and God's creation. Christians have traditionally affirmed that there's a radical difference between Creator and creation, between God and what God has created, and it's important for us to remember that difference.

Christians have also traditionally spoken of creation as being *ex nihilo* (out of nothing). We say that there was nothing before God created, only God, and so God alone is the source of everything that is, both spiritual and material. One of the reasons that Christians have always insisted on this teaching is that it rules out a rival god or gods. Evil is real, but its origin, as we will see in the next chapter, is in creation itself.

Dualism is still another heresy with which Christians have struggled from time to time. Dualism divides reality into spiritual and material components, and for dualists the spiritual is always good, while the material is always to be avoided. For a dualist, salvation can sometimes be understood as an escape from the material. And yet, the doctrine of creation tells us that God created everything — the spiritual *and* the material — and called all of it good. As we've seen, not only did God create everything, but he becomes real to us in the stuff of the earth. God became real to us, as we'll see, in the person of Jesus. Far from devaluing the significance of material things, God gave everything enormous value. And we human beings have been given the duty of caring for everything.

*   *   *

Here's another observation. The God we meet in these verses, the God with whom we have to do, is a welcoming God. The God of creation is hospitable, generous.

I sometimes like to ask confirmation classes why they think God created the heavens and the earth, and the answer I get most often — can you guess? — is that God was lonely. God needed someone to talk to, they say. And I'm not entirely sure where that idea comes from. My guess is that it comes from a high-school student's own projection about what God must feel.

But God wasn't lonely. God wasn't a needy being who decided to create a universe in order to satisfy inner needs that weren't being met. What the doctrine of creation teaches us is that God takes delight in sharing his glory. God creates because God is creative. Why does the artist draw? Why does the singer sing? Why does the poet write? Because that's what you do if it's in you, if it's in your nature.

God was not compelled to create the world. It is an act of free grace. Creation is a gift, a benefit.

Daniel L. Migliore, *Faith Seeking Understanding*

We learn something else about God by looking at creation. God is a risk-taker. God created us and this world in such a way that there was a possibility of rebellion. God gave us complete freedom to be ourselves within this creation, and we human beings have exercised the option. We'll talk more about where evil came from in the next chapter, the chapter on providence, but for now it's important simply to notice that God was willing to face the risk of rebellion. That's an astonishing insight into the nature of God.

In the sixteenth century, Andrey Rublyov painted what is now a famous icon. Maybe you've seen it or studied it in an art history class. The icon shows three angel-like figures sitting around a table, and the figures represent the Father, the Son, and the Holy Spirit.

In the painting, the Son is turned and is facing us, beckoning us. There is actually a space between the Father and the Holy Spirit, so that as we meditate on this icon, it's almost as though — and this is remarkable — we are being invited to take our place at the table, to share in the divine life.

This is what I think creation does. It invites us.

The Creator works in all things
    toward the new creation that is promised in Christ.

A Declaration of Faith, 1985 (PCUSA)

What the doctrine of creation teaches us is that, though we are creatures — fragile and vulnerable and susceptible to all kinds of disasters — we nevertheless belong to God. Our life is a gift, and that gift is sustained and preserved by God. Why? Because God loves his creation. God is passionate about you and me and everything that is. God invites us to offer our worship, to join in the praise. We have the freedom *not* to do that, of course, but the invitation is always there. In the end, it's what we were created to do. Creation invites us to respond.

* * *

On one of my rare trips anywhere (traveling to the hospital and back is what I call business travel), I was sitting on an airplane at the Dallas–Fort Worth Airport. The plane was full, everyone was buckled in, and we were ready to push back from the gate. I was ready for a couple of uninterrupted hours of reading, which for me is as good as it gets. Suddenly, I smelled smoke. And my first thought was, "Someone is clearly out of touch with federal regulations for domestic flights."

Almost as soon as I thought it, smoke started pouring out of the air vents. In seconds, the whole cabin filled with smoke, and I couldn't see a thing. I could hear the flight attendants saying, "Get out! Get out! Leave your carry-on luggage! Get out!" The exit doors somehow opened, and people started scrambling out onto the wings, of all places — and not always in an orderly way. There was a disturbing amount of screaming and shoving. I thought I was going to be trampled.

For just an instant I also thought about grabbing my bag out of the overhead compartment, in spite of the instructions, and then I said to myself, "I didn't come into this world with any luggage; I might as well go out that way too."

Well, obviously I survived to write this chapter, and as far as I know there wasn't a single injury, except maybe for some frayed nerves. But I had the feeling that I'm guessing we've all had at one time or another — "This is it. I'm done for."

Yet, here I am today, writing these words, and the overwhelming feeling I have is "Thank you." Not because God mysteriously intervened in creation to save my life, while deciding not to intervene in creation to save the lives of thousands of other people who have died in airline disasters over the years. (That's not the way God's providence works.) I'm thankful because, when I hear the story of creation in the first chapters of Genesis, I'm reminded once again that life is a gift. Sometimes it's long, sometimes it's short, but it's always a gift, and often it's an exceedingly beautiful gift.

*   *   *

God created the universe and all of us who are in it, and God called it good. God called *us* good. And furthermore, God gave creation a purpose; God gave *us* a purpose. And the purpose of creation, as I've said, is to glorify God.

The "chief end of man," as the Westminster Catechism put it long ago, is to glorify God and enjoy him forever.

And if you ask what it means to glorify God, I can answer best by telling you what one theologian has said: We glorify God by being alive, fully alive, by being all that we were created to be.

God gave you the gift of life, and now God is waiting for

your response, for your thank you. God is waiting for you to grab hold of life and to live it — with boldness and courage and thanksgiving. The God who created the heavens and the earth is a God of welcome and hospitality.

When you look at creation, how do *you* respond?

QUESTIONS FOR FURTHER STUDY AND REFLECTION

1. Some Christians believe that the biblical account of creation is in conflict with the modern scientific view. Do you agree? Why? Or why not?

2. What difference does it make that God created "the heavens and the earth"? What difference does it make that God and creation are separate and distinct from each other (if that's what you believe)?

3. Part of being thankful to God for creation involves genuinely embracing the gift of life. How do you do this?

What God Does

PART TWO: PROVIDENCE

Q. *What do you understand by the providence of God?*
A. Providence is
    the almighty and ever present power of God
    by which he upholds, as with his hand,
        heaven
        and earth
        and all creatures,
   and so rules them that
        leaf and blade,
        rain and drought,
        fruitful and lean years,
        food and drink,
        health and sickness,
        prosperity and poverty —
    all things, in fact, come to us
        not by chance
        but from his fatherly hand.

Lord's Day 10, Heidelberg Catechism, 1563

IF I WERE to tell you that the Bible is a love story, you might think that I was trivializing Scripture, putting it in the same category, maybe, as a romance novel.

Or you might begin to think of all those stories in the Bible that seem anything but loving. "What about Noah and the flood?" you might ask. "Or what about all those times when God ordered the people of Israel into battle, ordered them to utterly destroy cities and peoples?"

We're very skilled, I've discovered, at finding just the right counterexample. And that's good. What we believe should be able to stand up to the tough questions. In this chapter, however, I invite you to think of the Bible as a love story, as a record of God's loving relationship with his creation and his people.*

---

*My job would be easier if I could say, "Let's not deal with those annoying questions," and leave it at that. The truth is, people ask those questions just about every time the subject of God's providence is raised. So something ought to be said, though sorting through *each one* of those troubling Old Testament stories is beyond the aim of this book.

Whenever people raise questions about Old Testament history, I ask them to think with me about the way we read Scripture. The way we read (and interpret) Bible stories today is often very different from the way those stories were read (and interpreted) when they were first written. We bring some very different concerns and questions to our reading of the Bible. If we're going to use Bible stories to draw conclusions about God, I point out, then we need to do some interpretive work. We need to know some of the reasons those stories were remembered in the first place.

Old Testament scholars I know think it's important to read at least some of those difficult Bible stories with the category of holiness in mind. In other words, the people who wrote those stories most likely were not preoccupied with the same questions we are — how a good God, for example, could order the people of Israel to utterly destroy the people living in the land of Canaan. Our questions wouldn't have made much sense to them. Their concern was how a land that had become morally and spiritually polluted could once again be made holy. Seen through their eyes, the stories that often give us such trouble made a great deal of sense.

In a similar way, the category of holy war may help to explain other difficult Old Testament stories. When God orders the people of Israel into battle,

*   *   *

Speaking of trivializing Scripture, John 3:16 has never been as trivialized as it has been in recent years. I'm not talking about the words themselves, just the reference, which seems to show up at every golf tournament and football game held in the United States today. Somewhere at a sporting event this weekend, someone will probably hold up a sign with "John 3:16" on it.

I don't think much of that particular method of evangelism, but I do love the verse, which begins, "For God so loved the world that he gave his only-begotten Son. . . ." If you're going to do evangelism, you probably can't find a better message to start with than that one. And yet, the truth is, it's a tough message to sell. God loves the world he created. God loves you and me. But something about that truth is just plain difficult for most people to believe.

As I write this, one of the most popular weekly programs on network television is *Touched by an Angel*. Maybe you've seen it. Maybe you're even a big fan. Millions of people tune in each week, and they watch until, at some point (the real drama was *when*), they hear the punch line: "God loves you." Every week that thought just staggers the main character of that particular episode.

I once saw an interview with the producer of *Touched by an Angel*. There was the usual talk, of course, about how such an overtly religious program ever made it to network television in the first place, and then, in one of the most revealing parts of the interview, the producer was asked about that line: "God loves you."

What she said struck me. She said — and I agree with this —

---

often it's to rid a holy place of moral and spiritual impurity. Though perhaps not a pressing issue for us today, this was a very real issue to the writers of the Old Testament.

To sum up, the questions people raise today are good ones, but it's important to recognize that those questions reflect current sensibilities. When we read the Bible (and use it to bolster our arguments), we need to understand the issues and questions the Bible was written to address.

that all of us long to know we are loved. To be loved is one of the heart's deepest desires. And yet, she says, it's so difficult to accept that love when we find it or when we're confronted with it. And so the message of the show, in the memorable words of the producer, is "God loves you — get over it."

*　　*　　*

Question 8. How do you understand the love and power of God? Through Jesus Christ. In his life of compassion, his death on the cross, and his resurrection from the dead, I see how vast is God's love for the world — a love that is ready to suffer for our sakes, yet so strong that nothing will prevail against it.

The Study Catechism, 1998 (PCUSA)

Do you believe that? Do you really? Do you believe that God loves you?

I said those words to someone last week. "God loves you." It's not something I blurt out just anywhere — in a grocery store check-out line, let's say — but at the moment it seemed appropriate. I thought the person I was talking to needed to hear it. So I took the chance and just said it. "God loves you." And since she didn't feel very lovable — at least I'm guessing that's how she was feeling — she said, very matter of factly and without any hostility that I could detect, "If God loves us, then why is there so much suffering in the world? Why do children get sick and die? If God loves us, why does stuff like that have to happen?"

At that moment I realized why the doctrine of providence is such a tough sell in our world. Any time you mention God's ongoing care and concern for the world he has created, lovingly brought into being, someone somewhere is going to say, "Oh, yeah? Then why are things as bad as they are?"

*   *   *

In *Faith Seeking Understanding,* Daniel Migliore refers to the dramatization of this issue in a play by Tennessee Williams. In *Suddenly Last Summer,* there's a character named Sebastian, a young boy who is clearly searching for God. One day he's watching as some sea turtles emerge from their eggs and then try to make their way to the sea, which they need to do in order to survive. Just then some very large birds swoop down and devour most of the little turtles. Witnessing this carnage in what is a very powerful scene, Sebastian becomes hysterical, and he says to his mother, "Well, now I have seen Him!"

And of course he's referring to God.

Tennessee Williams and others like him believe that you don't have to look far in our world today to find evidence of cruelty and injustice. Even nature itself seems to exhibit senseless violence. For many people the evidence shows clearly that God doesn't care. How could God have designed a world in which this and more is possible?

Theologian Shirley Guthrie admits that this issue — the existence of evil or what he calls "the dark side of creation" — is a very "serious threat" to the Christian faith. I agree. You and I, if we're serious about our faith, if we're serious about being God's people in the world, should have an answer ready for this challenge. We should know what we believe.

*   *   *

The problem of evil is as old as creation itself, which is not to say that God created evil. In fact, that much we know for sure. God most certainly did not create evil or cause it to happen. That's one point I can't make strongly enough. God isn't the source of the evil in our world today — any of it.

I'll go one step further. God didn't create evil at the beginning, and God doesn't create it today. In spite of what some well-meaning Christian people sometimes say (and I hear them all the time, especially in the wake of a tragedy of some kind), God most certainly does not send evil or disease or suffering into our lives. I cringe whenever I hear someone say something like "God must be doing this for a reason."

Jane, the dear friend I mentioned in the first chapter, never once in all of my visits at the hospital blamed God for her illness. For her, the illness was an occasion for asking difficult questions, which is certainly a kind of testing. But she didn't believe that God gave her cancer so that she would grow in her faith.

God doesn't test us, at least not like that. God doesn't perform experiments to find out how much suffering human beings can tolerate. God wouldn't do that. What kind of a god would that be? The God we believe in is nothing like that.

Question 11. What do you understand by God's providence?
That God not only preserves the world, but also continually attends to it, ruling and sustaining it with wise and benevolent care. . . . In particular, God provides for the world by bringing good out of evil, so that nothing evil is permitted to occur that God does not bend finally to the good.

The Study Catechism, 1998 (PCUSA)

Let's say we think of God as a loving parent. (Remember that our language about God is always going to be limited.) Then what kind of a loving parent would cause suffering in the life of a child? What kind of parent would test a child to see what sort of endurance or faith that child had? It just doesn't make sense, does it? Intentionally causing pain or purposefully inflicting suffering in the lives of our children flies in the face of everything we feel as parents. If we are good and decent parents, we want only the best for our children, and most parents would sacrifice their own lives for the sake of their children if they had to.

And if that's *our* instinct as parents, then we can only imagine the motivation and desire of our God for us.*

*   *   *

Another claim that Christians make is this: Evil is real.

Maybe you already know as much from your own experience, so you don't need this reminder. But just in case there's any doubt, evil is a powerful force in our world, and evil has been a reality in the world almost since the beginning. There isn't a hu-

---

*Spiritual testing is an interesting topic, but I think it's different from the topic of this chapter. Over the years, many people of faith have reported times of spiritual testing in their lives. Difficult circumstances often cause people to rethink or reconsider their spiritual assumptions. What I'm rejecting here, I suppose, is the often-expressed idea that God would send a serious illness or death to a loved one as a way of determining the depth of our commitment to him.

It's true that in the prologue to the book of Job, God appears to be testing Job. And in the New Testament, we read that it was the Spirit who drove Jesus into the wilderness to be tested. So being tested by God may seem to have precedent in Scripture.

A careful reading of the Job story, however, reveals that it's really *God* who is tested, not Job. God boasts about his servant Job, and in response to that boast Satan issues a challenge. Job is faithful, Satan says, because he prospers. Take away the good things, Satan claims, and Job will quickly turn against his God. God accepts the challenge. In the end, it is Job who proves God right and Satan wrong. The story ends with God expressing wonder at the faithfulness of Job. God marvels at Job's ability to love, which is not the result of the good things Job enjoys from God.

Having said all of that, I must also admit that the evil Job suffers is real — and undeserved. If God didn't send it into Job's life, then clearly God allowed it to happen. Which is troubling and not easily explained.

The story of Jesus' testing falls into another category altogether, and may be interpreted as the sort of testing that all human beings encounter in life — Will we trust God to provide or won't we? What is remarkable about Jesus is that he chooses what we typically do not. In the story of the temptations, Jesus proves himself to be the kind of person we cannot, on our own, become. As the Epistle to the Hebrews puts it, Jesus was "one who in every respect has been tested as we are, yet without sin" (4:15).

man life that hasn't been touched by evil of some kind. All of us know and are familiar with evil in some shape or form.

Where did it come from? No one knows, though the story of the Fall in Genesis 3 is the biblical account of the origin of evil. What we do know for sure is this: God created a world where there was at least a potential for evil. Let me put this in a slightly different way, because it's a crucial point: Of all the possible worlds that God could have created (if you want to, you can imagine God looking at a variety of different designs before getting started, checking them all out, weighing the pros and cons of each one), God chose a world where you and I would be morally free beings.

God chose to create a world where human beings would be free, for example, to love — or not love. But loving or not loving would be our choice. And so, we believe that much of the evil which exists in our world today is a result of human choice (or human negligence). This is a critical point. You could say, I suppose, that we brought it on ourselves. And we keep on doing it too. That may not be pleasant to hear, but it's true. Examples of evil we bring on ourselves would include personal lifestyle choices that damage our health and industrial "accidents" that result in ecological catastrophes.

Human choice explains the existence of some but not all the evil in our world. Human choice does not, for example, explain why there are hurricanes and earthquakes and famines. Theologians sometimes refer to this category of evil as "natural evil." (A tornado itself is perhaps not evil, but the pain and suffering it leaves behind clearly are challenges to God's providential care.) Human choice also does not explain the existence of most natural evil such as disease. There is much about evil that we simply cannot explain and that we may never know. There is much about evil that is still a mystery and will perhaps always remain a mystery.

In an effort to explain — or at least understand — this mystery, some theologians have written recently about limitations to God's power. Since it's troubling, for example, to believe that God *could* intervene in our lives but chooses not to, there has been speculation that perhaps God's power is actually limited. These theologians would say that God wants to reach into creation and prevent certain instances of evil from happening — but can't.

An example of power that is voluntarily limited is parental power. When parents bring a child into the world (which is a form of creation), they must often make room for this child, and in doing so they often limit themselves. In fact, we *expect* parents to make space for their children, to allow their children to grow, to stand by them while they make sometimes-serious mistakes. Sometimes the most difficult part of parenting is knowing when to intervene and when to leave well enough alone. Could this be a sort of analogy to God's relationship with us? We don't know. Some people are deeply troubled by any suggestion that God's power is limited, but an all-powerful God who appears to do nothing when creation suffers raises other disturbing questions.

Maybe it's possible to say this much: The evil we experience in our lives, the evil that we wrestle with and feel the weight of — this is evil that God does not intend for us.

God intends just the opposite for us.

To speak of sin by itself, to speak of it apart from the realities of creation and grace, is to forget the resolve of God. God wants shalom and will pay any price to get it back. Human sin is stubborn, but not as stubborn as the grace of God and not half so persistent, not half so ready to suffer to win its way.

Cornelius Plantinga Jr., *Not the Way It's Supposed to Be*

At the beginning of biblical history, almost as soon as evil appeared, God was ready with a plan. From the beginning, we believe, God has been at work, renewing and restoring creation to its original state of "shalom," the way things were intended to be. The doctrine of providence is nothing less than the history or the record of God's efforts. God, for example, has always been on the side of the poor and the downtrodden. And that's why I mentioned at the beginning of this chapter that the Bible is a love story. God is at work in our world, pursuing us and wooing us back into relationship.

I recently heard Sister Donna Ayert, a Catholic theologian, speak about God's love for us in a way that I don't think I ever fully appreciated before. I've mentioned that God is like a parent, but there is some evidence in the Bible that God is also like a lover — a passionate, ardent lover who pursues us, wants us, and longs for us.

Ayert quoted from the Song of Solomon, a biblical book that isn't read in worship very often — perhaps because of our embarrassment over its content, its often-explicit sexual imagery. The book's meaning, though, is interesting to contemplate. What if the book is about God's relationship with us? What if God is just crazy about us and his creation, madly in love with all of it? You can read the whole biblical record, in fact, as the story of a sometimes unrequited lover.

How does that sound to you? For some of us, that may be an entirely new way of thinking about God and God's intentions toward us. If God is in love with his creation, then no wonder God won't let go of it. No wonder God will stop at nothing to reclaim it, to get it back. Our God — this is an astounding truth — is so passionate about his creation, so much in love with it, that he is ready to do whatever it takes — to humiliate himself, if necessary — in order to get it back.*

Christmas (I'll say more about this in the chapter on the Incarnation) is the story of what the Bible calls God's self-emptying. God gave up everything, everything that might matter to us, and God set it aside out of love for us. You name it — God

---

*Over the years Christians have spoken of the "humiliation" as well as the "exaltation" of Jesus Christ. His birth, life, and death were, in a sense, his humiliation, while his resurrection, ascension, and subsequent reign "at the right hand of God" were his exaltation. I have more to say about this in the last chapter on the Incarnation.

got rid of it. Power, privilege, status, ease, comfort, glory — in the birth of Jesus, God set it all aside. And how do you explain that (because it doesn't make sense in any logical sort of way), except to say that God was passionate about his creation, that God wanted to romance it?

Romance is one subject on which I don't claim to be an expert. I often feel terribly inept about it, but I know some of the fundamentals. And one of the fundamentals is that it takes a considerable amount of vulnerability to say "I love you" to another human being.

When *we* think about reclaiming creation, taking it back from the power of evil and restoring it to its original state of "shalom," I suppose we would think most naturally about a power struggle, a cosmic battle between the forces of good and evil. We would see God's role as overpowering evil in the world. And in fact we do find some evidence of that in the Bible, some talk of a cosmic battle or spiritual warfare. But the more I read the Bible, the more I get an altogether different perspective.

God's plan for reclaiming creation and setting things right again is to enter into it, to become a part of it. Sometimes God's presence is most deeply felt, most evident, not in good times but in times of our greatest pain and suffering. Sometimes God demonstrates his power not by subduing evil but by making good come out of evil (Gen. 50:20).

This is certainly the story of Jesus. Instead of destroying evil in a decisive battle, which is what we might expect of a mighty and powerful God, the God of Christian faith decided to become weak, to be born of a poor young woman, to grow up in near-poverty, to experience all the pain and disappointment that life can dish out, and then to die at the hands of the Roman government. Jesus' life, death, and resurrection teach us, among other things, that God demonstrates his power not in saving us from hurt but in sharing our hurt with us.

If you were to ask me why God did that, I would have to say that I don't know, but I have a good guess. Maybe the only way to break the power of evil in our lives is to meet it head on — on its own terms. Maybe the only way to make a real change in the world is to become vulnerable. Maybe — and this is just a guess — the best way God knows to get our attention and to be our God is to become one of us.

Do you see evidence of God's love in *your* life?

QUESTIONS FOR FURTHER STUDY AND REFLECTION

1. How do you respond to people who witness or experience a tragedy and say, "Why does God let this happen?" What do you say when Christian people try to accept evil as "God's will" for their lives?

2. If God didn't create evil, then where did evil come from? Was it an inevitable result of creation?

3. Christians believe in a personal God. What about a personal devil? Do you believe that there is a being named "Satan"?

Who Jesus Is

THE SECOND PERSON OF THE TRINITY

He comes to us as One unknown, without a name, as of old, by the lake-side, He came to those men who knew Him not. He speaks to us the same word: "Follow thou me!" and sets us to the tasks which He has to fulfill for our time. He commands. And to those who obey Him, whether they be wise or simple, He will reveal Himself in the toils, the conflicts, the sufferings which they shall pass through in His fellowship, and, as an ineffable mystery, they shall learn in their own experience Who He is.

Albert Schweitzer, *The Quest of the Historical Jesus*

WHO WAS JESUS? Who is Jesus for us today? Those are questions a believer should be able to answer. Can you?

Not long ago I was reading about a group of theologians and Bible scholars who call themselves the Jesus Seminar. According to news reports, they met together to review the sayings of Jesus in the Gospels and to determine which ones are authentic. Their findings? Most of Jesus' words, as we have them today, were actually put into his mouth by later believers. Other words attributed to Jesus are problematic, they decided, but may be close to something he actually said. And finally, a very small number of Jesus' words are probably authentic.

The Jesus Seminar received a great deal of publicity for their work, and the reaction from Christians to their work has been decidedly mixed. Some people, predictably, are outraged by the whole enterprise and find it hard to imagine a single good reason to engage in such work. Others claim not to know what's at stake and wonder what all the fuss is about. And still others — those in the middle — have started either to ask questions or to express doubts.

"Are these people on to something?" I've heard church members ask. "Should we be paying attention to what they say?"

John Dominic Crossan, a New Testament scholar, has provided leadership to the Jesus Seminar, and he has written several books about Jesus. Those books may not be representative of the thinking of all members of the group, but they may offer a good starting point for understanding the current debate about Jesus. One thing seems clear: There are people today who are asking pointed and sometimes disturbing questions about Jesus. Who *was* he? And who is he for us today?

Crossan presents Jesus as a social revolutionary with a message of what he calls "radical egalitarianism." In one of his parables, Jesus spoke about a person who gave a feast, but discovered that all of his friends had good excuses for not coming (Luke 14:15-24). So the would-be host sent servants into the streets to invite anyone at all. The result — frightening to contemplate in first-century culture — would have had males reclining at table with females, free people next to slaves, ritually pure next to ritually impure, socially high next to socially low, and so on. Jesus' message, Crossan contends, represented a serious challenge to the social order of his day. For Crossan, the Kingdom of God that Jesus envisioned and proclaimed was primarily a new social order.

Why [Jesus'] existence was so unsettling on every side was that He set all programs and principles into question. And he did this simply because He enjoyed and displayed, in relation to all the orders positively or negatively contested around Him, a remarkable freedom which . . . we can only describe as royal.

Karl Barth, *Church Dogmatics,* IV, 2, 171

Crossan says a great deal in his books about this egalitarian and revolutionary Jesus, and just about all of it is outside traditional Christian teaching. Crossan doesn't believe, for example, that the New Testament describes a physical or bodily resurrection of Jesus, as traditional Christian teaching maintains. Furthermore, he believes that dogs and birds of prey ate Jesus' crucified body, the usual aftermath of a Roman execution.

Crossan's claims are startling. His books are engaging. He clearly knows his New Testament. But anyone who wants to have a conversation with him, or with any of the Jesus Seminar scholars, should know something about traditional Christian teachings.

How did scholarly thinking about Jesus ever get to this point?

*   *   *

From the beginning, Jesus' true identity has been hotly debated. He seemed to sense the confusion himself when he said, "Who do people say that I am?" The answers the disciples gave ranged from "Elijah" to "John the Baptist." No one outside Jesus' small group seemed to have it right. So he pressed the issue with those who knew him best. "Who do *you* say that I am?" And Peter, often the first to speak, said, "The Messiah of God."

But I wonder how confident he really was of his answer. And what do those words really mean?

Early Christians struggled to find the language to say exactly what they believed about Jesus. Even those who knew him, who knew what he looked like and what he sounded like, who knew his family, had trouble agreeing on the best words to use. Coming to an exact description of Jesus, one on which there would be a broad consensus, took the early church hundreds of years.

Which is not to say that early Christians didn't work hard at the project and that their first efforts weren't any good. On the contrary, the earliest attempts to find language to describe Jesus are staggering, mostly because of how quickly the ideas about Jesus developed and how sophisticated the concepts became. One of the earliest of the Christian confessions about Jesus took the simple form "Jesus is Lord" (1 Cor. 12:3). John's Gospel, by contrast, was probably written several years later and gives evidence of swift advances in thinking and reflecting about Jesus. This is especially so in the prologue (John 1:1-18), where Jesus is described as the eternal Word or Logos, present with God at the creation. Since Jesus himself said little about his pre-existence, the description in the Fourth Gospel is all the more important to consider.

The Epistle to the Hebrews also contains some interesting insights about Jesus, dramatic and appealing ways of thinking about him and his mission. The earliest readers of that epistle were just beginning to contemplate what sort of person could be "like us in every way," except for one crucial characteristic — he was "without sin."

More than three hundred years went by, however, before Christians finally agreed on a common language. In 381, at the Council of Constantinople, the Nicene Creed came to its final form, and only then was the church able to say with any sort of unity what it believed. The largest single section of the Nicene Creed is about the second person of the Trinity, and each word there is carefully chosen and addresses a particular concern about Jesus' identity.

In the years before the Nicene Creed was written, there were those who believed that Jesus was divine and only appeared to be human. There were also those who believed that Jesus was human and seemed to act now and then in a divine or inspired sort of way. There were those, moreover, who believed that Jesus was born human but that at some point in his life (at his baptism, for example) God's spirit entered into him. All of these beliefs, and others like them, were eventually discarded or labeled as heresies. Instead, the church agreed to think of Jesus as fully divine and fully human, both at the same time. Jesus had two natures, both in the same person. That language, while still problematic,* seemed to describe best the Jesus who is described in the Bible.

Did this "two natures, one person" language end all of the debates? No, but at last the church had a way to talk about the person without whom there is no Christian faith.

*   *   *

What the Jesus Seminar is trying to do is get back to the beginning. These scholars are trying to peel away the layers of tradition

---

*Theological conversation about Jesus today continues to explore the issue of how the two natures are related. The traditional formula is that the two natures (divine and human) are "hypostatically" united in one person without confusion, change, division, or separation. Theologian Daniel Migliore describes the problem that many critics see in this teaching by referring to "two boards . . . glued together." Many thinkers would prefer a newer, less wooden way of understanding precisely how Jesus' two natures are joined together, while others are content to live with the paradox — or what they might call the mystical union of his person. See Daniel L. Migliore, *Faith Seeking Understanding: An Introduction to Christian Theology* (Grand Rapids: Wm. B. Eerdmans, 1991), pp. 149-50.

Question 21. Who is the Redeemer of God's elect?
The only Redeemer of God's elect is the Lord Jesus Christ, who, being the eternal Son of God, became man, and so was, and continueth to be, God and man, in two distinct natures, and one Person.

Westminster Shorter Catechism, 1647

and uncover Jesus as he actually existed — not as later believers came to think of him. These scholars are trying to find the real flesh-and-blood human being instead of the Jesus often represented in religious art.

Jesus Seminar scholars aren't the first to make the attempt. The quest for the historical Jesus has an interesting history of its own. The quest seems to have begun in earnest in the eighteenth century, when European intellectuals such as Voltaire thought it might be a good idea to apply the scientific method to the study of the Gospels. Since then, quite a number of quests have been undertaken over the years.

Maybe the best-known person to write a quest was Albert Schweitzer. Most people today remember Schweitzer as a white-haired doctor who spent his later life in the jungles of Africa, where he founded a medical clinic. Few people seem to know that before he became a doctor, Schweitzer was a skilled theologian (and a fine musician too). His best-known theological book is *The Quest of the Historical Jesus.* In it he concludes that the quest ultimately doesn't go anywhere. You can look all you want, he seems to say, but you're not going to find him. It's like looking down a well, he remarks at one point. In the end, all you see is your own reflection.

All previous quests for the historical Jesus have found not Jesus but a person who looks and sounds remarkably like the person who conducted the search. Voltaire found a Jesus who was virtually indistinguishable from an enlightened eighteenth-century Deist, and scholars today find a Jesus who matches up remarkably well with their own cultural biases and political agendas.

And who wants to believe in a savior like that? We want the real thing, don't we? We want the Jesus who is so appealingly described for us in the New Testament.

What do we learn there?

The best place to start is to consider seriously what the Gospels say about him. Matthew, Mark, Luke, and John are maddeningly quiet on certain details. They don't tell us all we want to know about his childhood, for example, but they do give us some amazing bits of information. Here are a few important ones:

First, Jesus was a first-century Jew. He wasn't a generic, featureless human being. He came to us as a member of a specific racial-ethnic group. And not just any racial-ethnic group, but a group that has experienced ridicule and oppression since at least the first century. That was no accident. Since God (as we've seen in a previous chapter) is always on the side of the poor and downtrodden, why would God act differently in the sending of the Son? Jesus came to us as a Jew.

We don't know what he looked like, but chances are good that he had all or most of the physical characteristics of the people with whom he lived. I'm suspicious of any art or film that portrays Jesus with blue eyes, pink complexion, or British accent. That's not who he was. But then maybe the Gospels are silent about his appearance because in the end it doesn't matter what he looked like.

Second, Jesus was a male. As one theologian puts it, "Real human beings are normally either male or female. Jesus was a male." He was circumcised on the eighth day, as were all other Jewish males. Until the late twentieth century, most people didn't make all that much of Jesus' gender, but lately both men and women seem to be taking a close look at what Jesus' gender might mean. I've been at large men's gatherings, for example, where popular contemporary preachers (all male) have described Jesus as the ideal male role model. Using the Gospels, they describe what they see as the specifically male characteristics of Jesus, and then of course they urge men today to change their lives accordingly.

I'm not sure exactly what to make of this thinking. Maybe there are men today who really want to hear that it's possible to be a man of integrity, compassion, and love — and still be thoroughly masculine. Maybe that's a strong need in our world today, where gender roles are confusing at best. But we must remind ourselves that that's a tricky path to take. It would be wrong to make an idol out of Jesus' gender. It would be wrong to make too much of his maleness.

He is the long-awaited Savior,
fully human and fully divine,
conceived by the Spirit of God
and born of the virgin Mary.

In the events of his earthly life —
his temptations and suffering,
his teaching and miracles,
his battles with demons and talks with sinners —
Jesus made present in deed and in word
the coming rule of God.

*Our World Belongs to God: A Contemporary
Testimony,* 1988 (CRCNA)

Most Christian thinkers over the years — and this is true of New Testament writers as well — have emphasized Jesus' humanity, not his maleness. Jesus shows us — and I mean all of us, men *and* women — what it looks like to be a human being. Jesus was the first human being after Adam and Eve to demonstrate perfect love for God and other people. There's nothing strictly masculine or feminine about that. What's so attractive about Jesus is that he came to us as a human being, that he was Emmanuel,

God with us. We ought to be suspicious of any preaching or teaching that calls attention to Jesus' gender. He was born a male, true enough, but he was the representative of a new humanity, not the archetype of maleness.

Third, Jesus experienced every human need and desire and limitation that we do. The more I reflect on this truth, the more astonished I become.

In Sunday school I was taught that Jesus was perfect, and in my youthful imagination this meant that he was some kind of superman: Jesus was bigger and faster and stronger than anybody else; Jesus hit a home run every time at bat; Jesus clubbed a hole in one from every tee; Jesus had perfect scores on all of his scholastic aptitude tests; and finally, Jesus never had to practice the piano because it somehow came naturally to him (in a way that it never came naturally to me).

But guess what. That's not what we believe. Jesus didn't know everything. He wasn't able to do everything. He didn't always know what everyone around him was thinking. He experienced limitations and finiteness. Luke's Gospel tells us that Jesus had to grow in stature and wisdom. In other words, Jesus wasn't just pretending to be a human being; he *was* a human being in every way that we are — except for one big difference. Jesus lived a morally pure life.

I find it helpful to see that Jesus was a product of his family of origin and surrounding culture, just as we are the products of our families of origin and also the cultures in which we live. One of my favorite Gospel stories is the one known as "Jesus and the Syrophoenician Woman." In that story Jesus came into contact with a woman who was a Gentile (Mark 7:24-30). Jesus' contemporaries would have thought of this woman as a "dog" — a familiar term of condescension for someone who was not a Jew.

Jesus actually came close to using this term himself. In response to her request for a healing, he said, "Let the children be fed first, for it is not fair to take the children's food and throw it to the dogs." And yet the word he used there, in the original language, sometimes has the meaning of "puppy." It sounds to me as though Jesus used this word with a wink, acknowledging the barrier that existed between them, and she apparently heard the verbal wink, too, because she answered with growing confidence, "Sir, even the dogs under the table eat the children's crumbs."

What happened in the story — in addition to the healing — is that Jesus went beyond what his culture had conditioned him to do. His stance of love enabled him to transcend prejudice. He was tempted to express himself as everyone else did, but he didn't do it. He demonstrated that it is possible to be human and to respond in love, even when that might not be our first impulse.

Finally, Jesus was a dangerous human being — "dangerous" in the sense of unpredictable or unconventional. People who are unpredictable and unconventional are often dangerous, and Jesus certainly was.

He dared to be on the wrong side of just about every issue. He dared to disappoint his family and friends for the sake of his calling, and every single one of them *was* disappointed by the end of his life. He dared to question the religious assumptions of his day when it would have been easier to keep quiet, but he didn't, and earned himself the label "blasphemer" for his trouble. He dared not just to be a friend of sinners (a tough enough job for us); he dared to forgive sinners.

*   *   *

Who was Jesus? He was fully human, as we have seen, but also fully divine.

Second Corinthians 5:19 says it clearly: "In Christ, God was reconciling the world to himself." Our trust isn't merely in a human being, as extraordinary as that human being was. No human being by himself or herself can do what needs to be done for us. But God can, and God was acting in Jesus on our behalf, as we'll see in the next chapter. Every time Jesus spoke, every time Jesus acted, it was God who was speaking and acting through Jesus.

QUESTIONS FOR FURTHER STUDY AND REFLECTION

1. For centuries the church struggled to say precisely who Jesus was and is. From your own reading (of this chapter, the Bible, and other sources), can you say who Jesus was and is for you?

2. Karl Barth, one of the most important theologians of the twentieth century, wrote that the exclusion of a human father in the story of Jesus' conception is important. Much of history is told as the story of males (statesmen, warriors, explorers, philosophers, kings, etc.), but in the most important event in history, the male is excluded. A woman named Mary becomes the primary agent of God's work in the world. What do you make of this interpretation?

3. What does it mean that Jesus was "without sin"?

What Jesus Does

ATONEMENT

Theories of atonement are an attempt to articulate a mystery, an experience of having been graciously dealt with by God. . . . They seek to express in limited, analogical language the reality of God's decisive act on behalf of a broken world. There was some kind of victory that took place, some kind of power shift in the universe, some kind of ransom paid, some kind of healing initiated, some kind of ultimate love displayed, some kind of dramatic rescue effected.

Leanne Van Dyk, *Dialog*

WHAT DOES IT MEAN to you that a man you never met, who lived two thousand years ago in another culture, and who spoke a different language — in other words, who doesn't have very much in common with you — what does it mean that *this* man died for you? What does it mean that he died for me? Or for any of us? What possible difference could that death make in your life and in mine?

These are not rhetorical questions. Christians should be able to give confident and specific answers to these questions.

After all, what Jesus did and still does for us lies at the very heart of the Christian faith. Jesus' death on our behalf is the good news that we call the gospel. And yet, for many of us there are few other teachings or doctrines that are quite as difficult to accept or embrace as this one. Even the Apostle Paul, in the middle of the first century, realized that what Jesus accomplished in his suffering and death would be foolishness to most people — "foolishness to the Gentiles and a stumbling block to the Jews" is how he put it.

Think about it. The church seems like a good idea, at least in the abstract. A group of well-meaning people commit themselves to love each other and other people. What's not to like about that — except, of course, particular churches? For most people the church is non-threatening, and sometimes it even sounds attractive.

Christian values fall into this same category. I'm thinking about fairness, truthfulness, and generosity — those who have sharing with those who do not. Who can object? We want our children to know and embrace these values and others like them, don't we? Once again, for most people there isn't anything all that threatening about Christian values.

I would even go so far as to say that a belief in God is non-threatening to most people. God — even the idea that God created the heavens and the earth — isn't an idea likely to provoke much of an argument.

When we get to the subject of this chapter, however, everything changes. What Jesus does on our behalf, described in the doctrine of the atonement, is a teaching without which we do not have a Christian faith. And yet, it is a teaching that has always been difficult to accept. Even some theologians, as we'll see, struggle to make sense of this teaching.

Christians believe that at the center of human history stands an event so awful, so violent, that no responsible parents today would allow their young children to watch it. And furthermore, we believe that this event, a fairly standard Roman execution, has eternal significance for our lives. Because Jesus died on that cross, we believe, our lives are different today, and they will be different for eternity. Because Jesus died on that cross, something is different about the universe itself.

In Christ, God was reconciling the world to himself,
   not holding our sins against us.
Each of us beholds on the cross
   the Savior who died in our place,
   so that we may no longer live for ourselves,
   but for him.
In him is our only hope of salvation.

A Declaration of Faith, 1985 (PCUSA)

Theologians call what Jesus did atonement. Actually, theologians have a fairly large number of different terms for what Jesus did, all describing different facets or dimensions of Jesus' work: expiation, redemption, justification, reconciliation, and so on. I'm using "atonement" here in its broadest, most inclusive sense.*

---

*What Jesus does for us can be described with a variety of words, but so can the process of salvation itself. Christians have traditionally thought of their salvation as a series of stages. One recent list I saw includes the following: we are elected, called, illumined, converted, regenerated, justified, mystically united with Christ, sanctified, preserved to the end, and glorified with the Son.

An innocent or sinless person dies, or somehow gives his life, so that a sinner can go free. That's atonement, or more specifically that's *substitutionary* atonement. An innocent or sinless person makes things right for a guilty person. Some people wrestle with this, and they end up saying, "It just doesn't make sense. It's like kicking the dog because of the mess the cat made. It's not fair."

Or they will say, "I'm not that bad, and God isn't that mad."

In recent years certain feminist theologians have objected to the doctrine of atonement in part because it seems to promote or condone abuse. As they see it, the Son dies while the Father looks on, and it appears that the Father is not only giving his permission but expressing his satisfaction. It's possible, they say, to come away from this teaching with a distorted view of God, a God who is sadistic and angry. In an article about the Father's relationship with the Son entitled "Divine Child Abuse?" Joanne Carlson Brown claims that Christianity is "an abusive theology that glorifies suffering."

What do Christians say in the face of such a critique?

It's true that *some* pastors over the years have wrongly counseled battered women to "bear their cross" and to "be imitators of Christ." It's true that *some* women have been wrongly encouraged "to obey and submit" to violent and abusive husbands or partners. It's even true that parts of the Christian faith have been used in some unfortunate ways. But the feminist theologians I have in mind here, several of whom are prominent and influential thinkers, have gone a step further and concluded that something is wrong with this idea of atonement and therefore with the Christian faith itself.

Is atonement an idea that still makes sense today?

* * *

A philosopher of religion named John Hare has written a book recently called *The Moral Gap*. In it he too wrestles with this idea of atonement. He asks the same question that I've raised in this chapter: Does it make any sense that someone could have died in our place? And here's what he says. Atonement is actually a common experience in our lives. Atonement, he writes, is something that happens all around us, in various forms and at various times.

He gives a number of examples.

One is of a corporate merger or takeover. When a larger corporation merges with or takes over a smaller corporation, all of its debts, liabilities, pending lawsuits, and customer dissatisfaction become the responsibility of the larger corporation. Whether they like it or not. Whether they were fully prepared for it or not. Whether they deserve it or not. It happens. That's a form of atonement. Even the Bible, it's interesting to notice, clearly uses a financial image to describe what Jesus does for us (e.g., Mark 10:45; Rom. 3:24; 1 Cor. 6:20 and 7:23; Gal. 3:13; Titus 2:14; 1 Pet. 1:18).

Adoption is another of Hare's examples. When a family adopts a child, he writes, there's a merging of identities, and the adopting family assumes whatever the child has brought into the family, both assets and liabilities. And sometimes the liabilities can appear to outweigh the assets. But that's the meaning — and the risk — of adoption. The Bible, too, makes it clear that Christians are adopted sons and daughters of God.

Other biblical examples of atonement include the sacrificial image and the legal image. In the New Testament the sacrificial image makes reference to the Old Testament practice of sacrificing animals, especially lambs, to remove human guilt. Jesus takes the place of the lamb and is "sacrificed" as an atonement for our sins (Rom. 3:25). The legal image makes use of courtroom characters such as judge and defendant, as well as terminology such as "verdicts" and "justice." Jesus is often viewed as the innocent person who takes the place of the guilty defendant (e.g., Rom. 5:6-11; 2 Cor. 5:16-21; Col. 1:19-20).

No single image by itself can adequately explain the doctrine of the atonement. As theologian Leanne Van Dyk puts it, "Theories of atonement do not claim to define or explicate the inner mechanics of salvation. Rather, they suggest images of

> To say that Jesus' love cost him his life means, in plain words, that He was so much for us, and that we meant so much to him, that He suffered through our human lot with us and that He wanted to be at our side precisely when we were guilty, and when we must suffer and die.
>
> Helmut Thielicke, *I Believe*

how salvation is effective." Our language may be limited, but the reality behind the language is still good news for a broken world.

*   *   *

Not long ago I had the opportunity to see the film *Sling Blade,* which won some well-deserved Academy Awards the year it was released. The film concerns a man who is released from a state hospital after having lived there for twenty years. He then goes to live with a family who generously take him in, allowing him to become part of their lives. Almost immediately, however, we begin to see that the family is terribly dysfunctional. There is even something that feels evil or demonic in the household.

At the end of the film, it is the mental patient who offers himself, *sacrifices* his life, for the sake of this troubled family. You could say that he saves them when they can't save themselves. He gives up his own freedom and happiness so that they can have life. In a sense, the central character in *Sling Blade* is a Christ figure. The method he chooses to save his host family is violent, but it is still arguably a form of salvation for them.

Christ figures are common not only in life but also in film and literature.

*   *   *

As I thought about this subject and tried to make sense of it for myself, it occurred to me that one of the reasons the atonement is hard to accept is that we aren't always convinced of our own sinfulness. If we don't think of ourselves as bad people, then we're certainly not going to feel an urgent *need* for atonement. God's saving work in Jesus Christ isn't going to make much sense unless we have a healthy regard for the presence of sin and evil in our world — and, more specifically, a healthy regard for the presence of sin and evil in our own lives.

How bad are things? Most days, to tell the truth, things seem pretty good where I live. We have our moments, of course — everybody does. But in general can you really call things bad?

Maybe it's the insidious nature of evil that allows us to ask a question like that. Our world is so far from what God intended it to be, so far from the "shalom" of creation, that we don't even have a reference point anymore. Good? What's good? Somehow it's possible for us to look evil in the face and not even recognize it for what it is. Somehow it's possible to look at our lives and not see how far short of the glory of God we fall.

God looks at the world he has made, and he grieves. God remembers what he intended for us, and he grieves. God sees what we do to each other — not just what we're conscious of, but those things we're not even aware we do — and God grieves. How bad is it? God thought it was bad enough. Read the Old Testament sometime, or just the book of Genesis. God was beside himself when he saw the way his creation was turning out.

"I know the world *out there* has problems," we might say to ourselves, "but how bad am *I*?"

Most days I don't seem so bad. I like to give myself high grades. To myself I seem okay. Most days. But let me try to make one change in my life, let me try to fix one area where I need to improve, or let me work on one behavior that I'm not very proud of — and I find it next to impossible to make a change.

Not because I don't have inner strength or a strong will. I have both of those. But most of the time it's nearly impossible for me to make changes in my life, even relatively minor ones. And in spiritual terms — I'm not sure what you'd call it in psychological terms — we call that sin. The good I want to do? I don't do it. And the bad stuff I don't want to do? That's exactly what I do. And so with the Apostle Paul I say, "Wretched man that I am." With the tax collector in Jesus' parable, I say, "God, be merciful to me, a sinner." Without God's help, without God's intervention on my behalf, there's no hope for me.

*   *   *

There is nothing but God's grace. We walk upon it; we breathe it; we live and die by it.

Robert Louis Stevenson

When I think about the doctrine of atonement, I see three truths. I think these truths are absolutely essential for Christian people to grasp if we're ever going to understand what the atonement means for us.

The first truth is *grace*.

In Jesus' well-known parable of the Pharisee and the Tax Collector, the first person to pray is the Pharisee, who tries very hard to justify himself. He offers to God a rather impressive list of reasons why God should love him and consider him worthy. How many of us can say that we fast twice a week — for religious reasons? Or how many of us can say that we tithe 10 percent of our income — gross, not net? How many of us can say that we do both — fast *and* tithe? If you had asked the Pharisee whether or not sin was a big problem in his life, he might have said, "Not really. I'm doing okay. Got it under control. Had some problems years ago, maybe, but not today. Truth is, I'm not that bad."

Truth was, his sinful nature had blinded him to honest self-appraisal. He was clueless. He wasn't aware of his pride and conceit, but they were obvious to everyone else.

The second person to pray is the tax collector. His prayer is simple. He's a sinner, and he knows it. He doesn't even promise to do better next time — perhaps because he knows better than to make a promise like that.

So, "which one is right with God?" Jesus asks.

The answer is that the tax collector is. Why? Because we can't make ourselves right with God. No amount of tithing or fasting is going to make us acceptable to God. Ultimately, there isn't anything we can do — except to throw ourselves on the mercy of God and be grateful for what God has already done for us in Jesus Christ. We don't deserve it, but we get it anyway. And that's grace.

* * *

Here's a second truth. In the atonement God teaches us something about the nature of *forgiveness*. What's truly remarkable is that it's the injured or aggrieved party here — God — who reaches out to restore the relationship.

All you have to do, to remind yourself how remarkable that is, is to think about most human relationships. Most of us, when we're hurt, want nothing more to do with the person who hurt us. We would never make the first move, at least not willingly. We'll listen, maybe, if the person who hurt us comes crawling to us, but being the first to reach out, being the first to act, taking the initiative — that's godly love, and it's seldom something we experience with people we know.

It is this truth, more than any other I have heard, that sets Christianity apart from most other world religions. The God we believe in has always taken the initiative with us. The God of Christian faith wants us, desires us, and will not rest until we respond.

* * *

Here's one last truth. We're talking here about costly *love*.

If God loves us and forgives us, then why did somebody

91

have to die? Why didn't God just say, "I love you. Now why don't we just let it go at that?"

That's a good question, and it deserves an answer.

Think one more time about most human relationships. What happens when you go to someone and say, "I'm sorry, I'm truly sorry, for what I did," and then that person says, "Oh, that's okay — it doesn't matter. Just forget it"? That doesn't feel much like forgiveness, does it? It doesn't, especially if the wrong we've done is very serious.

Being told to "forget about it" may be a kind of forgiveness, but it sounds too much like, "I don't care enough about you to be bothered by anything you say or do. You're just not that important to me." God's response to us is very different.

Real love, real forgiveness, means caring enough to be hurt, caring enough to feel the pain and brokenness in the other person and to want to remove it — no matter what the cost. That's what Jesus does for us. No matter what the cost.

*   *   *

Whenever I think about what God has done for me in Jesus Christ, whenever I think about the grace involved, and the forgiveness, and the costliness of the love — I don't know what to say. I don't have the words to describe what I feel. All I know is that my life can no longer be the same. I am so grateful. To be loved and forgiven in this way — it's the best news I've ever heard. Nothing I've ever known comes close to this. I have experienced the grace of God in my life.

Let me ask you something. How do *you* respond to something like that?

QUESTIONS FOR FURTHER STUDY AND REFLECTION

1. In this chapter I mention that an acknowledgment of our sinfulness is important if we are going to sense the need for atonement. Do you think of yourself as a sinner? What's healthy about acknowledging our sin? Are there unhealthy ways to acknowledge it?

2. If Jesus' death on the cross was the decisive event in history that Christians claim it was, then why are sin and evil still so pervasive?

3. Can you think of examples of atonement from art and literature — or from your own life?

Who the Holy Spirit Is

THE THIRD PERSON OF THE TRINITY

As the wind is thy symbol
so forward our goings.
As the dove
so launch us heavenwards.
As water
so purify our spirits.
As a cloud
so abate our temptations.
As dew
so revive our languor.
As fire
so purge out our dross.

Christina Rossetti,
"To the Holy Spirit"

A FEW YEARS AGO, in a memorable ABC News program about religious trends in America, news anchor Peter Jennings interviewed John Wimber, who is probably best remembered for his role as a singer with the Righteous Brothers.

As Wimber engagingly told the story, his singing group had long since disbanded, and he was a recovering heroin addict who was looking for spiritual meaning in his life. One Sunday morning he wandered into a Presbyterian church in southern California. After a couple of Sunday mornings at the same church, Wimber approached an usher and asked, "When do they do the stuff?"

Puzzled, the usher replied, "What stuff?"

And Wimber said, "You know, the stuff — the stuff that Jesus did, like healing the sick, restoring sight to the blind. That kind of stuff."

The usher's response — and the punch line to Wimber's story — was, "Oh, we don't do that stuff here."

After a few chuckles, Wimber described how he then founded a church of his own, known as the Vineyard Fellowship. This church has grown dramatically, and today there are Vineyard Fellowships all over North America. Wimber's conclusion, clearly supported by film footage of large Christian gatherings in both the United States and Canada, was that many people were hungry for "the stuff that Jesus did."

*   *   *

In the late sixties and early seventies, the Christian church experienced what some people have called a "charismatic renewal." Pentecostal Christians — those who speak in tongues, practice faith healings, exorcise demons, and so forth — have been around for a long time, but this was something new. The charismatic movement seemed to take hold in nearly every denomination, even those like my own that are not traditionally associated with charismatic styles of worship.

As historians have reflected on what happened, they seem to agree that many people were looking for something more than they had been experiencing in their worship. To these people church often felt like a vast bureaucracy, and for them worship was often stiff and formal, with very little life and exuberance. They wanted more than that. They wanted to experience God alive within them. And charismatic worship seemed to provide what they were looking for.

Wherever the Holy Spirit comes to a person he comes . . . to fill, not only to effect; to dwell, not simply to visit. . . . Finally, the Holy Spirit is a person, and therefore where he is, he is fully, and not two-thirds or three-quarters.

Frederick Dale Bruner,
A Theology of the Holy Spirit

Though there is no such thing as *typical* charismatic worship, some common elements you might find would include people raising their hands to pray and sing, speaking in the New Testament language called glossolalia (also known as "speaking in tongues"), witnessing or experiencing physical healing, and claiming to have been baptized in the Holy Spirit. Interestingly, a large number of churches that broadcast their worship on television, I've noticed, include some or all of these elements in their broadcasts.

Other Christians often don't know what to make of those who emphasize the role of the Spirit in worship. Presbyterians, for example, pride themselves on, among other things, doing things "decently and in order," and so to them charismatic worship styles often feel jarring. Beyond that, charismatic Christians themselves sometimes say that *all* Christians need to give evidence of the Spirit. It's not enough, they say, to go to church, to pray, and to be involved in mission. They maintain that Christian people need to manifest gifts of the Spirit in their lives — especially such obvious gifts as speaking in tongues.

To Christian people I know — to members of my own church, for example — these are disturbing claims. Neighbors or people they know from work will ask them if they would like to be "baptized in the Spirit." Often implicit in these invitations — and sometimes explicit — is the sense that this is what real Christians do. If they were *real* Christians, they would speak in tongues.

What should we say to fellow Christians who make these claims? How should we understand the role of the Spirit in worship as well as in other areas of our lives? What do Christians believe about the Holy Spirit?

One helpful (and sympathetic) way to understand the charismatic movement is to look at it historically. It grew out of an earnest desire to experience God as personal, though clearly the desire was more than that. The movement grew out of a longing many Christians had to experience God as personal *and* powerful, personal *and* mysterious, personal *and* alive, just the way God is described in the New Testament book of Acts. Maybe Christian worship in some places had become stiff and formal, cold and lifeless. Maybe the charismatic movement was, in fact, a much-needed *renewal* movement for the Christian church, reminding all of us of some truths about God we had forgotten or neglected.

When we speak about the Holy Spirit, for example, we don't speak simply about a God "out there" or a God who acted "way back in history." When we speak about the Holy Spirit, we are speaking about a God who is immediate and accessible. Not simply a God who is near us, but a God who is *inside* us, a God who animates and transforms our lives. Maybe that was a reminder Christian people needed to hear.

Another response we might make to those who say all Christians should manifest gifts of the Spirit is to look at the movement in more personal terms. In other words, maybe we should simply agree. If we're people of faith, we *should* be giving evidence of the Spirit's presence in our lives; we *should* be able to point to "gifts of the Spirit."

The question is, What would that look like?

In Paul's first letter to the Corinthians (especially chapters 12–14), he has a great deal to say about gifts of the Spirit, primarily because the Corinthian church was having its problems with spiritual gifts. These would be helpful chapters for all Christians to read, since they speak directly to the importance of the Spirit's work in our lives. Maybe the most important truth to be found there is Paul's claim that we are all given different gifts to use "for the common good." In other words, there are many gifts, but they are distributed among us so that we all have a contribution to make.

Some, Paul writes, are given the gift of being apostles; others, the gift of being prophets; still others, the gift of being teachers. In fact, the list of gifts is a long one. It includes gifts having to do with leadership and healing as well as speaking in tongues. Then Paul asks some rhetorical questions: "Are all apostles? Are all prophets? Are all teachers?" And so on. What's important, Paul seems to imply, is not that we all give evidence of the same gift (speaking in tongues, let's say), but rather that, taken together, these gifts enrich the community, making it greater than the sum of its parts.

O God our Father, who sent your Son to be our Savior: renew in us day by day the power of your Holy Spirit; that with knowledge and zeal, with courage and love, with gratitude and hope, we may strive powerfully in your service.

William Temple,
Archbishop of Canterbury

Finally, in 1 Corinthians 13, Paul describes "a still more excellent way." Which turns out to be love. Not a sentimental feeling, not romantic love, but *agape* love — the kind of selfless, sacrificial love demonstrated by Jesus himself. Of all the gifts of the

Spirit, this one is the greatest, and without it, everything else is "nothing."

Later in the New Testament, in Paul's letter to the Galatians (5:22-23), we also read about "the fruit of the Spirit," and there is the sense in these verses too that if the Spirit is in you, then you're going to exhibit evidence of it. People are going to notice it in you. "Love, joy, peace, patience, kindness, generosity, faithfulness, gentleness, and self-control" — these are the signs, Paul writes, that the Spirit of God is within you. The opposite of the fruit of the Spirit, as Paul sees it, are "the works of the flesh" (Gal. 5:19-21). It's one or the other.

*   *   *

Here's something else that's important to remember about the Holy Spirit. It's a tough, nearly impossible job to say what the Spirit is. It's much easier to describe what the Spirit has done in or among us than to say what exactly the Spirit is. It's also much easier to say where the Spirit has been than to say where exactly the Spirit is now.

William Willimon, in a recent Pentecost sermon that I found particularly helpful, said that trying to describe the Spirit is a lot like trying to describe fire and wind, two biblical metaphors for speaking about the Spirit.

This is how Willimon put it: If someone tried to describe fire by saying, "Well, first I smelled smoke, then I heard the sirens, and finally I saw a red glow in the sky," we might say, "That's not fire. That's smoke, sirens, and a red glow, but that's not fire." Similarly, if someone tried to describe wind by saying, "Well, there was a rustle of leaves, then I heard the wind chimes, and finally, somewhere in the house, I could hear a door slam shut," we might say, "That's not wind. That's leaves in the trees, clanking metal, and a door slamming against its frame, but that's not wind."

Willimon went on to say that, in the end, we have to describe the Spirit in the same terms, by mentioning its effects, by pointing to what it does in us and through us. The Holy Spirit is a mystery, and descriptions like these just might be as close as we can get to saying what we mean.

At Pentecost the Apostle Peter was filled with the Holy Spirit, but the description we read in the book of Acts mainly concerns the effects of the Spirit in Peter. Here was a man who had only a modest education at best and what appeared to be a limited potential for leadership. Beyond that, his apprenticeship in ministry was exceedingly brief. And yet, after being filled with the Holy Spirit, as the story puts it, he stood in front of a large crowd in Jerusalem and preached the sermon of his life. Three thousand people were "cut to the heart" by what he said and formed a movement that was to become the church, a movement that was to engulf the whole Roman Empire.

That, we might say, was the Holy Spirit. Someone else, however, might say, "That's not the Holy Spirit. That was a man who somehow rose to the occasion. Courageous and moving, maybe, but not the Holy Spirit."

But to people of faith, this description of the Holy Spirit may be the best description we can have. Think of the creation story. In many ways it's similar. In Genesis 1:2 we read that "a wind from God swept over the face of the waters." It was then that God's creating power became evident. The whole universe came to life. That wind, we believe, was the Spirit of God. And think of Genesis 2:7, where we read about the creation of the first human being. God fashioned a man out of the clay and, as the story puts it, "breathed into his nostrils the breath of life." It was then, in the words of the story, that "the man became a living being." He came to life. That breath, too, was the Spirit of God.

Christians would say that this is the way of the Holy Spirit. The formless void, the lump of clay, the Galilean fisherman named Peter — in each case the Spirit appeared and delivered the gift of life.

*   *   *

101

Q. *What do you believe concerning "the Holy Spirit"?*
A. First, he, as well as the Father and the Son,
   is eternal God.

   Second, he has been given to me personally,
       so that, by true faith,
       he makes me share in Christ and all his blessings,
       comforts me,
       and remains with me forever.

Lord's Day 20, Heidelberg Catechism, 1563

Here's another way of thinking about the Holy Spirit. According to the New Testament, if we want to know who the Spirit is, we are to look at Jesus. Jesus and the Spirit are connected in two important ways.

First, it was Jesus who received the Spirit (Matt. 3:16) and carried it around with him, so that it was in the Spirit that he healed the sick, cast out demons, and brought good news to the poor (Luke 4:18). The Gospels seem to say that if you want to know who the Spirit is and what it looks like to have the Spirit within you, then look at Jesus. In the words of one theologian, he is our "prime example" of what it means to be a Spirit-filled person.

What is appealing to me about this is that Jesus didn't fit the definition of a *spiritual* person — at least not for the religious people of his day and probably not for the religious people of our day. His behavior repeatedly raised the eyebrows of those who thought they knew how a good, religious person should act. Jesus liked to have a good time. He went to parties where there were all kinds of people — including morally suspect people. He ate with them and talked with them. More than that, he defended them. He seemed to go out of his way to demonstrate love and compassion to such people. Finally, his life choices did not "pay off" in terms of material or popular success. Just the opposite was true. By the end of his life, he was despised by most people, and he disappointed his few remaining friends.

The deep irony of the Bible is that *this* person was a Spirit-filled person.

Second, Jesus wasn't only filled with the Spirit himself; he also promised the coming of the Spirit to his disciples. In John 14–15, in his parting words to the disciples, Jesus announced that he would send an "Advocate" or "Spirit of truth." The purpose of the "Advocate" was to teach, to remind the disciples what Jesus himself had said: "The Holy Spirit, whom the Father will send in my name, will teach you everything, and remind you of all that I have said to you" (14:26).

$$* \qquad * \qquad *$$

Here's a final thought. Theologians sometimes speak of the Holy Spirit as "re-presenting" Christ to us. Which is a reminder, I suppose, that we are dealing here with a trinitarian God, not some separate and distinct being. When the Holy Spirit re-presents Christ to us, it's as though the Spirit closes the gap of space and time. Because of the Holy Spirit, Christ isn't just a memory or someone who is coming back someday. Because of the Holy Spirit, Christ is present with us — here and now.

As John Calvin puts it, it's in the "energy of the Spirit" that we come to "enjoy Christ and all his benefits."

How is the Holy Spirit is alive in *your* life?

QUESTIONS FOR FURTHER STUDY AND REFLECTION

1. Many Christians have felt the need for a more personal faith — one they feel as opposed to one they merely think about. How does the Spirit help Christians develop a more personal faith?

2. How prominently does the Spirit figure in your own faith? Or devotional life? Do you ever pray to the Spirit?

3. When other Christians challenge you to ask God for the gift of "tongues" or to receive the "baptism of the Holy Spirit," what do you say? Why?

What the Holy Spirit Does

THE CHURCH

Q. *What do you believe concerning "the Holy Catholic Church"?*
A. I believe that the Son of God
    through his Spirit and Word,
    out of the entire human race,
    from the beginning of the world to its end,
  gathers, protects, and preserves for himself
    a community chosen for eternal life
    and united in true faith.
  And of this community I am and will always be
    a living member.

Lord's Day 21, Heidelberg Catechism, 1563

IF YOU ARE A CHRISTIAN, then you have been called to a new way of living alongside and in partnership with other Christians.

I was tempted to write that to be a follower of Christ means you link up with other followers, but putting it that way almost makes the partnership seem optional. The truth is, to be a follower of Christ *is* to be a partner with other followers. There's no other way to think of it.

Long ago the church had an expression for this belief, and in Latin it was *extra ecclesia nulla salus*. That's better known to us today as "outside the church there is no salvation." Now, to us, of course, that expression just smacks of heavy-handedness, something we don't like to associate with the church. But — this may come as a surprise to you — the church has never backed away from that claim.

The church still says that when you announce your faith in Jesus Christ as Lord and Savior, you have at that moment aligned yourself with every other human being, living or dead, who ever made that profession of faith. When you announce your faith in Jesus Christ, you become, whether you know it or not, a part of the church.

In this chapter I intend to say in more detail what it means to be part of the church — part of a particular church, but also part of the church as it exists throughout the world and as it has existed throughout history.

What does it mean to be part of the church today?

*   *   *

John Buchanan, pastor of Fourth Presbyterian Church in downtown Chicago, has written a book about the church called *Being Church, Becoming Community*. At one point in the book he describes an unusual Sunday morning in his life and how it became a kind of epiphany for him.

John was on vacation, but he had to return to Chicago for some family business and ended up spending Saturday night at

106

home. As he describes it, waking up Sunday morning and not having to lead worship was a disorienting experience. He wasn't sure exactly what he was going to do with himself, so he slipped into the balcony at Fourth Presbyterian's early service and listened to one of his staff members preach. Then he climbed on his bicycle for a long ride along the lake.

As he rode along, he says, he felt like a tourist in a strange land. Three free hours on a Sunday morning was an undiscovered country for him. He saw people — lots of them — who were clearly not heading for church and who were enjoying themselves immensely. It was a beautiful day to be alive in downtown Chicago!

Finally, he pulled in to a cafe he'd heard about, ordered an omelette, and began to read a discarded *New York Times* — and then, he writes, the question occurred to him. And this is how he puts it:

> This is wonderful! I thought. What luxury! What a beautiful city! What a great way to spend a Sunday morning! Why would anybody want to do anything else with the exquisite gift of a free and pleasant morning in Chicago than be on the lake front, drinking coffee, reading the newspaper, waiting for a delicious Denver omelette?

What has become increasingly clear is that many, many people have asked themselves the same question, and they've answered it by staying away from the church. People today stay away from the church in droves.

Recent studies show that worship attendance is at a low point in this country — at least since the days when people started keeping records like these. The numbers spiked briefly during the war with Iraq, what researchers called the "Desert Storm Effect." But overall, it's as though the bottom has fallen out of worship attendance all over the country. The nineties in general have not been kind to the American church.

Do you know the reason most people give for their lack of

participation in a church? It's not that they're too busy — at least that's not the reason they give to researchers. It's that the church is irrelevant to their lives, or that the church too often fails to deliver what it promises.

Among those who say they're at least open to the idea of participating in a church, researchers detected a disappointment or even a feeling of betrayal. Too often, people say, the church just isn't what it claims to be.

A member of my church who rarely misses his weekly AA meeting likes to say to me, "You know, Doug, sometimes an AA meeting feels a lot more like the church than the church does. *We* put the New Testament into practice, and that's not what I experience on Sunday morning when I go to church."

There shall always be the Church and the World
And the Heart of Man
Shivering and fluttering between them, choosing
    and chosen,
Valiant, ignoble, dark and full of light,
Swinging between Hell Gate and Heaven Gate.
And the Gates of Hell shall not prevail.
Darkness now, then
light.

T. S. Eliot, *The Rock*

One theologian has called this the "scandal of particularity." And what he means is that the church is a good idea in the abstract. But church as it actually exists is just plain embarrassing.

As long ago as the Middle Ages, the church wrestled with this problem — what we strive to be and what we actually are — and the church invented language to describe it. Perhaps you've heard before about the "visible" and the "invisible" church.

The visible church is the church we can all see, the one that occasionally embarrasses us. We say one thing and do another. We talk love and practice something else. The invisible church is the ideal that always seems to be just out of our reach.

John Calvin was never happy with talk about the visible and the invisible church, even though his own church in Geneva fell far short of the ideal. The church, he said, can never exist merely as an ideal; instead, he preferred to think of the church in process. We're not there, but we're getting there — slowly sometimes, painfully, but always striving to become the church that God is calling us to be.

First Peter 2:9-10 ("you are a chosen race, a royal priesthood") has this sense of striving about it. If you read the surrounding verses, you get the sense that Peter is writing to a group of people who could be something more, who *want* to be something more. And so he's exhorting them, challenging them to become what they were intended to be. Historically, Christians have said that it's the Holy Spirit who calls and equips us to be the church.

The question, I think, is how we do that. How do we become more than we often are? How do we begin to make the invisible visible in our life together?

*   *   *

Secrets and Lies is a film that helped me to understand this issue better. It's set in England and examines class distinctions in that country. The film introduces us to a black woman, Hortense, who is an optometrist. She has a university education and works in an office. She even has a desk of her own. Obviously she has made something of herself. At a certain point in her life, though, she decides to find her birth mother. What she discovers is that her mother is white, which is something of a scandal, at least in the context of the film.

As it turns out, the birth mother and her family haven't done as much with their lives. They don't show much evidence of having been educated. They don't have offices or work at desks. Their table manners leave a lot to be desired. And so there's clearly a class difference between Hortense and her biological mother's family.

What's interesting, though, is that as the film moves along, the family raises itself. They start to act and talk differently. In the presence of this new family member, they become something more than they were. It's almost as though they see in this daughter, sister, and niece they didn't know they had what might be possible for themselves. In a wonderful way, she turns out to be good for them.

The connection I see between that film and the church is simply this: It's Jesus Christ who is at the center of the church's life, and in his presence we too become more than we often are. We see him, and we realize that more is possible for us, more is expected. And so we raise ourselves. Not all at once, maybe, but bit by bit, slowly, as we spend time in his presence.

*   *   *

Christians have always believed that the church exists where Jesus Christ is in the center. The way people have known that a particular church was really the church was by looking for what they called the marks of the church. And the marks of the church have always been the preaching of the Word and the celebration of the sacraments. When you have those two things, we believe, you have the church of Jesus Christ.

Wherever we see the Word of God purely preached and heard, and the sacraments administered according to Christ's institution, there, it is not to be doubted, a church of God exists.

John Calvin,
Institutes, 4.1.9

The marks of the church are important to remember, and people who call themselves Christians should be aware of them and look for them.

Why would we come out to church on a beautiful Sunday in Chicago or anywhere else? To answer John Buchanan's question, it's to put ourselves in the presence of Jesus Christ and to be changed by him, to raise ourselves and become better than we ever imagined we could be. It's not that worship is a kind of self-improvement course; it's that in worship we discover who we really are. God reminds us that we have a wonderful identity.

*　　*　　*

Eugene Peterson, a Presbyterian pastor and author, writes that the pastors of America have become a "company of shopkeepers," and the shops they keep, of course, are churches. They have become preoccupied, he says, with shopkeepers' concerns — like how to keep the customers happy, how to lure customers from the competitor down the street, and how to package the goods so that the customers will keep laying down their money.

Some pastors, he says, are very good, very adept at being shopkeepers. Some of them attract a lot of customers, pull in large sums of money, and develop good reputations in the community. And yet, Peterson says, no matter what you call it, it's still shopkeeping.

I think Peterson is on to something, but I'd go a step further. It's not only the pastors. It's the members themselves who use the language of consumers to describe the way we are together in the church:

- "Church shopping" seems to be the name people now give to the search for a church home. When people move to a new community, we typically say that they *shop* for a church that meets their particular needs, as though they're spiritual consumers looking for just the right deal. And of course the church that is successful is going to have just the right combination of products and services to meet their needs.

- When people leave church on Sunday, they'll often say to each other, "Did you get anything out of that today?" or "I didn't get anything out of that, did you?" as though worship takes place primarily to satisfy our own personal needs and preferences. Christians today seem to have forgotten that for centuries people have worshipped in order to offer themselves to God. The critical question used to be, "Is God pleased with what I offered (of myself) today?" Now the issue isn't so much what *we* offer to God; the issue for us has become *our own needs*. Were they met, or weren't they?

- Christians today often think of giving to the church as a kind of payment for services rendered. We give not always as a thankful response to the God who has so richly blessed us, but rather out of a sense that we're paying for things we need — youth programs for our kids, pastoral care for our shut-ins, and so on. And, well-trained consumers that we are, we want to get the best value for our dollar.

I could cite more examples, but I think these three make my point.

*   *   *

Something has happened to us. That's clear. In many places we've forgotten who or what the church is supposed to be. And pastors, as Eugene Peterson puts it so clearly, have helped to perpetuate our ignorance. The culture around us may be consumer-oriented, but we're called to be something new and different, aren't we? Aren't we called to be a new community, brothers and sisters in Jesus Christ, a communion of saints?

The work of the Holy Spirit is to call forth a new community. That's what Christians have traditionally believed about the Holy Spirit.

This may come as something of a surprise to us, since we tend to think of the Spirit's work almost entirely in individual terms — what the Spirit does *in me* — but the New Testament makes clear that the Spirit calls forth and equips the church to be the people of God.

The Greek word for "church" that appears throughout the New Testament is *ekklesia,* which is usually translated "called out." We are people who have been called out of culture, called out of the world in which we find ourselves, for the purpose of establishing something new, a community of faith.

*   *   *

When we say the Nicene Creed, we say that we believe in "one, holy, catholic, and apostolic church." For centuries, those four adjectives — "one," "holy," "catholic," and "apostolic" — have been central to our understanding of the church, but here I want to focus on just the last one — "apostolic."

What does it mean today to call the church "apostolic"?

Literally, "apostolic" means "in line with the apostles." But in the creed the word refers to the church's mission. Like the apostles and the saints before us, we have been sent forth to be God's people in the world. We have been both called out of the world and sent into it.

In the eighteenth and nineteenth centuries, sending people was relatively easy to do. Those were wonderful years for mission. The church sent people all over the world. And the good news is, all of that sending forth was fruitful. The church today exists in nearly every country.

By the middle of the twentieth century, though, something began to happen. Things began to unravel. We lost our sense of what it meant to be an apostolic church. We forgot what it meant to be a sending church. Most people that I know today find it hard to say exactly what it means to be an apostolic church.

Kennon Callahan, in a book called *Effective Church Leadership,* writes about the change we've experienced, and he uses the term "churched culture" to describe how things used to be and the term "mission outpost" to describe how things are beginning to look.

But you are a chosen race, a royal priesthood, a holy nation, God's own people, in order that you may proclaim the mighty acts of him who called you out of darkness into his marvelous light.

1 Peter 2:9

What Callahan says is that it's helpful for us to think of the church as a mission outpost in a hostile or at least an indifferent world. Life in a mission outpost, he says, is always precarious. Funding is always ready to run out. Resources — human and otherwise — are limited. In a mission outpost situation, you're always a generation or less away from extinction. But the exciting part of it is that you have a strong sense of mission or purpose in a mission outpost. You know why you're there, and the contributions of each person are absolutely essential.

What we need to recover, Callahan says, is this sense of a people on a mission. We are apostolic people — people who have been sent. And if we wonder where it is that we've been sent, the answer is, right here, wherever we happen to be. As a new century begins, our mission field, so to speak, is wherever we happen to be. As the mission committee at my church puts it, "Mission begins at our curb."

*   *   *

In chapter 20 of John's Gospel, we read that Jesus appeared to the disciples, who were gathered on the first day of the week behind closed doors. This could be a description of the church at worship. The disciples were frightened and unsure of themselves;

they were wondering about the future. They thought they knew what it meant to be a follower of Jesus, but with his death, everything changed. Their unspoken question was, "What's going to become of us?"

So Jesus appeared to them and said, "Just as God sent me to the world, now I am going to send you. You're going to be apostles."

Then, verse 22 says, he *breathed* on them. (Remember the Greek word for Spirit also has the meaning of wind or breath.) He said, "Receive the Holy Spirit," and he concluded with a statement about forgiveness. They were going to be a community based on forgiveness and love. Not dynamic programs, not interesting activities for people of all ages, but something more, something compelling and magnetic, something that would draw people in.

The Spirit came among them, and they stopped being a group of loosely connected individuals, each one wanting something different from Jesus, and they became a community on a mission. They started thinking of themselves as being on a mission from God, and they began to do extraordinary things. Empowered by the Spirit, they became a force in the world, a force that had no army, but a force that eventually took hold of the Roman Empire.

I pray for that same Spirit today.

QUESTIONS FOR FURTHER STUDY AND REFLECTION

1. Why is the church important? Why is going to church and worshipping with other Christians important?

2. "People of God," "bride of Christ," "body of Christ" — the church uses many different images to describe itself. What image is most helpful to you as you think about the church today? Why?

3. Give a definition of the church's task of mission and evangelism.

Becoming Like Christ

SANCTIFICATION

We believe Christ gives and demands of us
   lives in pilgrimage toward God's kingdom. . . .
Christ calls each of us to a life appropriate
    to that kingdom:
   to serve as he has served us;
   to take up our cross,
    risking the consequences of faithful discipleship;
   to walk by faith, not by sight,
   to hope for what we have not seen.

A Declaration of Faith, 1985 (PCUSA)

IF YOU HAD BEEN on the New York subway recently, you probably would have been doing what other subway riders were doing — namely, trying not to make eye contact with anyone else and instead reading the advertisements on the walls of the subway car.

One of the ads you would have seen — right next to the Finlandia vodka ad — would have been an ad with this large, in-your-face headline: **"Become a Loser!"**

Now, you might not have read any further — either because you already think of yourself as a loser (in which case you don't need further advice about how to become one) or because losing is not the trajectory of your life.

But, if that "Become a Loser" headline triggered something inside you, you might have read the ad's fine print, which said,

> If you're looking for the courage to give up the things in this world that keep you from being the best you can be, give us a call. We'll help you lose your old life and build a new one. After all, Jesus Christ lost everything, and he gained the whole world.

After reading that, you probably would have been hooked. You would have wanted to know who sponsored an ad like that. And so you would have read the even-finer print at the bottom of the ad, which said, "The Episcopal Church of the Heavenly Rest," followed by the address somewhere on Fifth Avenue, in Manhattan, the Upper East Side.

I give them credit. I don't know if it ever was especially easy to sell a message like that. But certainly today — in New York City as well as in Wheaton, Illinois, where I live — "Become a Loser" is a tough message to sell.

After the ad began appearing in subway cars around New York, a *Wall Street Journal* reporter called the pastor (or the rector) of the church to get more of the story. Actually, the church sounds a lot like the one I serve. The annual operating budget is similar, and so is the size of the congregation. And yet the ad campaign, according to the rector, cost around twelve thousand dollars a month — a hefty expenditure, in my experience, unless communicating a message like this is really where your heart is.

According to the Reverend James L. Burns, the rector at Heavenly Rest, "it used to be that everybody was a lapsed something. A lapsed Methodist, maybe, or a lapsed Catholic, or even a lapsed Episcopalian." There was a time, he said, when people could fall back on something in a time of crisis or as the need arose. But no more.

"Today," according to the rector, "very few young people get much of an exposure to religion in their childhood. And so, I don't know what else to do," he said, "except to start with the basics."

I think he's right about that. But what *are* the basics of living the Christian life?

There is nothing in the world as delightful as a continual walk with God.

Brother Lawrence, *The Practice of the Presence of God*

---

*   *   *

Not long ago I received an e-mail from a college student who's a member of my church. The message was a long one, and in it the student tried to tell me something about what his belief system was like after almost four years of college.

After growing up in the church I serve, attending its Sunday school, and participating in its youth programs, he was about ready to graduate and get a job. All of his training and education were about ready to pay off.

Can you guess what he said his personal mission statement was? This is what he wrote: "To live well, to do good to others, and to be happy."

When I read that, my first response was, "Well, it could have been worse. At least the 'doing good to others' sounds somewhat promising." I wanted to be understanding about this, after all, because I can remember some of the statements I made as a college student. They weren't nearly as harmless as this one, and I certainly wouldn't want to be held accountable for them today.

But later, after I had time to think about it, I felt a strong sense of failure. A sense of institutional failure — a sense that my church had let someone down — and a sense of personal failure, a sense that I had let someone down.

How is it possible for someone to grow up in a church like mine, go through all of the grades of our Sunday school, come in contact with all of the faithful people who are members, participate in the youth programs of the church — how is it possible to do all of that and then say, "My own security and my own happiness are two of the three most important causes in my life"? How is that possible?

Somehow — and I don't claim to know how — our children and youth are not getting or internalizing the very heart and core of the Christian faith. Somehow our children are growing up in the church but not feeling the radical claim of the gospel in their lives. And to me that's a serious matter.

"Living well" is not the issue here. I like to live well too. The issue is the goal or purpose of our lives. The issue is what we devote our lives or our energies to.

God Almighty, Eternal, Righteous, and Merciful, give to us poor sinners to do for thy sake all that we know of thy will, and to will always what pleases thee, so that inwardly purified, enlightened, and kindled by the fire of the Holy Spirit, we may follow in the footprints of thy well-beloved Son, our Lord Jesus Christ.

St. Francis of Assisi

---

*   *   *

Sanctification is the doctrine of the Christian faith that asks, Now what? Now that I can see how far the world is from the way it's supposed to be, now that I see how far *I* am from what I was created to be, now that God has decided to do something about it, now that Jesus Christ has come into the world and died, now that he gave his life for me — *now what?*

What's important to see is that God's work in Jesus Christ is only part of the story. It's the first part of the equation, so to speak. But there is more to the story than that. The rest of the story is what's required of us.

Dietrich Bonhoeffer, the German theologian who died at the hands of the Nazis at the end of World War II, will most likely always be remembered for his phrase "cheap grace." Cheap grace, he said, is what you have when there's little or no response to God's work in the world. Cheap grace is what you have when you hear of God's love in Jesus Christ and then don't do much of anything about it. We all know, he wrote, that God's grace is costly. And so, precisely because it is so costly, it demands a response from us. Otherwise, it becomes cheap grace.

The response God is looking for — this is something our tradition has always taught — is a process known as sanctification. Literally, the process of being made holy. God, you see, is looking for people who are going to grow in faith — or, to put it in New Testament language — people who are going to grow into "the full stature of Jesus Christ." Our response — or our mission statement in life — is to become imitators of Jesus Christ, who according to the Gospel narratives never once put his own comfort or his own security before that of anyone else.

*   *   *

In Philippians 3:14, the Apostle Paul writes, "I press on toward the goal for the prize of the heavenly call of God in Christ Jesus."

I like the way Eugene Peterson translates these words and

Becoming holy or sanctified in the New Testament sense means being conformed to the image of Christ by the working of the Holy Spirit in our lives. The essential mark of this Christ-likeness is that free self-giving, other-regarding love that the New Testament calls agape. Released from the compulsive power of self-centeredness, we are enabled to love God and our neighbors.

Daniel L. Migliore, *Faith Seeking Understanding*

the surrounding verses in his translation of the New Testament known as *The Message:*

> I'm not saying that I have this all together, that I have it made. But I am well on my way, reaching for Christ, who has so wondrously reached out for me. Friends, don't get me wrong: By no means do I count myself an expert in all of this, but I've got my eye on the goal, where God is beckoning us onward — to Jesus. I'm off and running, and I'm not turning back.

Paul is describing sanctification. In a sense, he's giving us his personal mission statement too. He's using himself as an example, and he's urging us to get going.

I see three dimensions to the Christian life as Paul describes it here: first, that it involves urgency; second, that it is a race, not a walk in the park; and finally, that there is a compelling goal, a destination toward which we're all moving.

First, the sense of urgency.

You can read these verses of Paul in any translation you want, but the clear sense in all of them is that when we talk about the Christian life, we're talking about an urgent matter. Paul intentionally uses the language of pressing forward, straining, and reaching. There is almost a feeling of breathlessness, isn't there, as you read these verses?

As I see it, we have a brief window of opportunity. At least that's what I see when I look at my own children as well as the children and young people of the church I serve. Our kids are growing up fast. And as they grow, they're making decisions about what's going to be important to them.

One option they have, of course, is to make themselves the center of the universe. That's certainly one way to live. Lots of people have chosen it over the years too. But there is another way to live. And that's what people of faith need to be talking about and living in a way that their children and young people can understand. They have the option, as that New York City ad campaign puts it, to "become losers." They have the option of giving themselves away.

If we make ourselves the center of the universe, however, we have to accept the consequences of that. We're choosing a way of life that's empty and shallow and void of meaning. And we become the prisoners of our own wants and desires. At one point in the recent film *The Truman Show,* the main character is sitting on a dock with the person he believes to be his best friend, and suddenly he asks, "Do you ever have the feeling that the whole universe revolves around you?" In the context of the film, it's a disturbing question. He asks because he senses that things are a bit off, not as they were intended to be. To be the center of the universe in this extreme way is not to be free. The paradox, as the film shows, is that it's a kind of imprisonment.

As I read it, the New Testament says that we find freedom by giving ourselves away, by finding the meaning in our lives *outside* ourselves. The culture around us is telling our kids a lie when it claims that their own happiness is all that matters. And who will tell them that's a lie if we don't?

But there's more. Paul describes the Christian life as a race. That's partly where his breathlessness comes from. Believers I have known like to think of the Christian life as a journey, a *leisurely* journey at that. Church people tend to think we're here to see the sights, when the truth is that we're here to run a race. Living the Christian life the way it's supposed to be lived means that we have to work hard, make an effort. There isn't anything about this that will come easily to us.

And finally, Paul talks about a goal, a destination toward which all of us are moving. And I think it's important to say exactly what that destination is — just so that there's no confusion.

The destination of the Christian life is not to be good people or good citizens, or even to be good parents, good husbands, good wives, or good children. Frankly, I wouldn't waste my energy in ministry if the primary goal of the Christian life were simply to become good, decent, caring, devoted people. Not that there's anything wrong with that. It's just that the goal we've been given is so much higher, so much loftier, so much worthier than that.

The destination, the goal of the Christian life is to be people who are becoming like Christ, people who are imitators of Christ.

*   *   *

I suppose I could choose any one of a number of aspects of life to get specific about the way we're supposed to live the Christian life. I could choose vocation, for example. Too many people have forgotten that our work isn't just a job; it's a calling. I could choose marriage, family life, or even leisure. By talking about money, though, I'm in very good company.

When I have any money I get rid of it as quickly as possible, lest it find a way into my heart.

John Wesley

Jesus talked more about money than he did about any other subject. He knew that money plays an enormous role in our spiritual lives. It plays an enormous role in how we set our personal priorities.

Recently I received a letter from a family that had been members of my church. Last summer they relocated from Wheaton to another part of the country. Before they left, I mentioned a church I knew in their new community and encouraged them to visit. The pastor is someone I know well, and I thought they would like him and respond to his ministry.

They went, which was good news to me, and recently they mailed me a copy of the church bulletin — and a pledge card. The family from our church, as it turned out, had gone on Pledge Sunday or Stewardship Sunday, as this day is variously known.

In the letter they mentioned how nice the church was and how friendly the people were. And then they said, "We went on Pledge Sunday. Ha, ha. And heard their stewardship sermon. Well, I guess we'll have to go again next week to get a better impression of the kind of church this is."

And I thought, "Well, if you can't get a good impression on Pledge Sunday, you never will." When people talk about money, you know exactly where they are spiritually. That's as close to the center of their lives as you can get.

We give our money (or our time) partly because we want to support outstanding programs in the church or in our communities. But it seems to me that we give primarily because giving is what people of faith do. People who are becoming like Christ, people who are in the process of sanctification, are by definition grateful people. We give because we don't know how to hold back. We see the example set for us in Jesus Christ, and our lives are filled with thanksgiving.

We also give because everything we have is ultimately a gift from God. We earned it, in a sense, but only in a sense. Everything we have we hold in trust. We are stewards of everything in creation and of creation itself. And so giving reminds us that what we have doesn't really belong to us, at least not in any lasting way.

I'll mention one more reason we give. We give because of the spiritual discipline of giving. Giving — like praying, like reading the Bible, like fasting, like any of the classical spiritual disciplines

— is a way of practicing holiness. It's a reminder that we are utterly dependent on God. We may like to think that our lives depend only on ourselves, but the person of faith knows better.

Progress in sanctification never meant working out one's salvation under one's own auspices; on the contrary, it meant working out one's own salvation with a rising sense of dependence on God's grace.

G. C. Berkouwer, *Faith and Sanctification*

A while back I read a story in the newspaper about the Arthur family in Wilmington, Delaware. I'm not sure why the Associated Press considered this story newsworthy, but I think it was so strange, so unusual, that it warranted a long article.

The Arthurs, according to the story, could live in a nicer house than they do. But they don't. They could drive nicer cars than they do. But they don't. Instead, they give about half of their pretax income to the church and other charitable causes. Their household income is about $80,000 a year, close to what the average household income in Wheaton is. That means their monthly income as a family is about $6,600. And yet, every month, Judy Arthur, who pays the bills, writes checks totaling $3,300 to a variety of causes they as a family have decided to support. In addition to mom and dad, there are two teenagers in this household who are affected by these giving decisions.

Why do they do it? Sam Arthur, the father, has a simple answer: "God has always blessed me." Apparently he's a man of few words, and that's his reason.

While he was a student at the University of California at Berkeley twenty-five years ago, he started to read C. S. Lewis, the well-known Christian writer. Through his reading, he learned that Lewis gave away 65 percent of his income. "That challenged me," Sam Arthur recalled, "and I decided then and there to give

50 percent of my own income away." That was the mission statement with which he graduated from college.

I grew up in a household where tithing was just something we did. I learned at a young age to set aside a portion of my income each week or each month. And like all children, I figured that all families did pretty much the same thing. As a young adult, I quickly learned how different we were from other families. My family modeled something for me — a spirit of generosity — for which I am grateful.

I sometimes feel very proud of myself and my giving habits, and then I'll read about the Sam and Judy Arthurs of the world, and I'll realize how far I still have to go. If the Christian life is a race, as the Apostle Paul says it is, then I'm actually somewhere very close to the starting line. I'm just now getting started. Which, I suppose, could be discouraging. But — and this is the good news for me — I see the goal. I know where God is calling me.

The question for all of us is, Now what?

QUESTIONS FOR FURTHER STUDY AND REFLECTION

1. In the Heidelberg Catechism, the title over the Ten Commandments is "Thankfulness." How is keeping God's law an example of thankfulness?

2. Read James 2:14-26. What's the relationship between faith and works?

3. When Dietrich Bonhoeffer talked about "cheap grace," what was he warning against? What's the relationship between grace and sanctification?

Object Lessons in Grace

THE SACRAMENTS

God meets us in the sacraments,
holy acts in which his deeds
elicit our response.
God reminds and assures us in baptism . . . .
that his covenant love saves us,
that he washes away our guilt,
gives us the Spirit,
and expects our love in return.
In the supper our Lord offers
the bread and cup to believers
to guarantee our share
in his death and resurrection,
and to unite us to him
and to each other.
We take this food gladly,
announcing as we eat
that Jesus is our life
and that he shall come again
to call us to the Supper of the Lamb.

Our World Belongs to God:
A Contemporary Testimony, 1988 (CRCNA)

GOD MEETS US in the sacraments. What do we mean when we say that?

One theologian says that all of creation is, in a sense, a sacrament of God. Nicholas Wolterstorff, who teaches at Yale University and who has written about worship in the Reformed tradition, says that for Christian people to think sacramentally is the most natural stance we can take. And that's true, he says, because we believe that reality itself is drenched in the sacred.

Christians also believe that worship itself is intrinsically sacramental. Why? Because in worship we take the stuff of creation — the water of baptism, the bread and wine of communion — and we believe that they become for us the vehicles of God's grace, bearers of Christ to us. God becomes present to us in them.

I know people who like to say that the Catholic Church and certain other Christian denominations are sacramental, meaning that they emphasize the sacraments in their worship by celebrating them every week, while a church like mine does not. They would say my church is not sacramental in this sense. And though there's a level at which this claim is true, worship by its very nature, by definition, is sacramental. God becomes present to us in the stuff of creation. God meets us in the sacraments. The worship at my church, therefore, is sacramental.

*   *   *

What's supposed to happen — not what *does* happen, but what is *supposed* to happen — when we participate in the sacraments?

Remembering is one of the things we do when we participate in the sacraments. When we say, for example, that the water of baptism and the bread and wine of communion are vehicles of God's grace, we're not saying that God's grace comes to us automatically or magically, as if we don't need to think about it very much. There are some things that have to happen — and one of those is remembering.

130

When Moses in Exodus 13 gives instructions to the people of Israel about how to celebrate the Passover, he says each celebrant should take the bread and then say to the children, "I'm doing this because of what the Lord did for me, when I came up out of Egypt" (13:8).

He was the word that spake it,
He took the bread and brake it;
And what that word did make it,
I do believe and take it.

John Donne,
"On the Sacrament"

And so, for generations, people who have participated in the Passover have made this statement of memory. "I do this because of what the Lord did for me, when I came up out of Egypt." Not because they were physically present, but because the bread represents the act. It becomes real to those who participate. The bread becomes a vehicle of God's saving act, and people today can participate in it, even though the Exodus from Egypt happened a long time ago.

To capture the true meaning of the word "remember," think of its opposite. Which would be "dismember," I suppose. If you were to *dis*-member something, you would tear it apart. So when you *re*-member something, you could say that you pull it together, you re-knit it. That, we believe, is what happens to us when we celebrate the Lord's Supper. At the table we say, "Christ has died, Christ is risen, and Christ will come again." We call all of that to mind, we become part of it, and we say that Christ becomes real to us. We remember it as if we were there, because in a way, in an important way, we *were* there.

*   *   *

131

In some churches, especially Roman Catholic ones, you often see small bowls of water at the entrance to the sanctuary. If you watch closely as worshippers enter one of those churches, you sometimes see them dip a finger or two into the water and then make the sign of the cross on their foreheads. Only then do they enter and find a seat. What they're doing in that small act of preparation for worship is remembering their baptism.

The sacrament of baptism confers a special identity on those who are baptized. That identity has to do with belonging. In a sense, baptism is a rite of initiation. In baptism we are welcomed into the church. And so the act of remembering one's baptism is really the act of remembering one's identity or one's membership. As worshippers enter the sanctuary, they are reminding themselves that, by virtue of their baptism, they belong to God and are part of a great company of other believers.

I do not remember my own baptism. My parents have described it to me, and they have occasionally pointed out the stooped, white-haired pastor who once sprinkled the water on my head, but I have no memory of being baptized — or of anything else that happened to me during the first year of my life. Even so, I *remember* my baptism daily in the sense that I reclaim my special identity as a child of God.

Every time I celebrate the sacrament of baptism, as part of the liturgy I ask worshippers to remember their own baptisms. When I do that, I don't expect that many of them will remember the actual event, but I hope they will remember (and reclaim) what happened to them when they were baptized. Actually, everyone is invited to participate in the sacrament. It isn't only for the baby or her adoring parents. Everyone who gathers to witness a baptism in worship is invited to participate in the act of remembering.

There's a story I've heard about Martin Luther. Every morning he would wash his face, and as he splashed water on himself he would say, "Martin, remember your baptism." Whether or not it really happened, I like to think it's true. I wish everyone who has been baptized would begin the day by looking in the mirror and seeing there the sign of the cross. We have all been marked as Christ's own.

*   *   *

Remembering can seem very passive, but as I think about the sacraments — or the way we participate in them — they're anything but passive. They require something from us. And what's required isn't only our remembering but our participation.

In his first letter to the Corinthians, the Apostle Paul addressed a question about whether or not it was acceptable to eat meat sacrificed to idols. The people of Corinth, including the new Christian community there, were worldly, sophisticated people. Corinth was an important commercial center, and clearly the temple feasts were an important part of community life. If you didn't participate, you missed something. The problem was that the meat served at these gatherings had been used in sacrifices to pagan idols.

Q. *What are sacraments?*
A. Sacraments are holy signs and seals for us to see.
    They were instituted by God so that
    by our use of them
    he might make us understand more clearly
        the promise of the gospel,
    and might put his seal on that promise.

    And this is God's promise:
    to forgive our sins and give us eternal life
        by grace alone
        because of Christ's one sacrifice
        finished on the cross.

    Lord's Day 25, Heidelberg Catechism, 1563

Nobody much believed in those ancient ceremonies anymore; participants valued the social connection. Understandably, the Christians in Corinth wanted to stay connected to their community. "We don't believe in it, anyway," they said to Paul in chapter 8, "so what harm can there be in it?"

But Paul wrote, "Think it through with me for a minute. I'm talking to reasonable people here. Let's remember what we're doing in the sacrament." And he reminded the Christians in Corinth that in the sacrament we become linked to Christ. "The cup of blessing that we bless," Paul wrote in chapter 10, "is that not a sharing in the blood of Christ? And what about the bread that we break? Is that not a sharing in the body of Christ? Don't you see?" he asked. "In the sacrament we have become one body."

The Greek word he used in this context is *koinonia*, which is probably a word you've heard in church before. It's an important word in the Christian vocabulary. *Koinonia* means "fellowship," of course, but it means something more. Not merely fellowship, not merely friendship, but deep personal bonds. When we come together in the sacrament, we experience *koinonia* — not only with God but also with each other. And Paul responded the way he did to protect the integrity of those bonds.

So here was his question: "How can you be partners both with God and with demons? It doesn't make sense. You can't sit at one table and then sit at the other. Make up your minds. To whom are you going to be joined? To Christ — or to someone or something else?"

The sacraments — and this is true of both the Lord's Supper and baptism — demand from us a pledge of allegiance, an oath of loyalty. Participation makes clear where we stand. In some churches, including the one I now serve, worshippers get out of their seats and go to the front of the church to receive the elements, and one of the reasons is that, in doing so, we make a public declaration of what we believe.

In my tradition we don't have what some Christians call "altar calls." You could say, I suppose, that we don't need them because we have the sacraments. Every time we celebrate the sacraments, we are saying in the most public sort of way exactly what we believe. The sacraments call on us to take a stand — not once but often, as often as every week.

I wish we celebrated the Lord's Supper with more frequency than we do. I don't know about you, but I sometimes forget from week to week which side I'm on. I join myself to Christ on Sunday and then to "demons," as the Apostle Paul puts it, the rest of the week. Weekly celebrations would push me to declare myself. I could say, "I'm sorry. This week I forgot who I was. Last Sunday I pledged my loyalty to Jesus Christ, and on Tuesday I had a . . . well, a memory lapse. Before I knew it, there I was, eating in the temple and thinking, 'What can it hurt, really, to eat a little of this meat?' So today, I renew my pledge."

Even the word *sacrament* has this element of pledge to it. In Latin, the word *sacramentum,* which is where our word *sacrament* comes from, refers to a pledge the Roman soldiers made. They swore an oath of loyalty or faithfulness to Caesar. We do the same thing when we participate in the sacraments. We say exactly which side we're on. We bind ourselves to God and also to each other.

*   *   *

The Apostle Paul has a great deal to say about the sacraments — and the sacrament of the Lord's Supper in particular — in his first letter to the Corinthians. When word reached him about worship in the Corinthian church, he was concerned, maybe even appalled, and rightly so. He fired off this letter to warn them about some of the things they were doing.

In a way it was good that they were having problems, because otherwise we might never have known how important the subject was to Paul. When he wrote letters to the other churches, he didn't mention the sacraments nearly as much. But the problems in Corinth have become an opportunity for us to learn about the sacraments in the early church.

Question 68. What is a sacrament?
A sacrament is a special act of Christian worship, insti-
tuted by Christ, which uses a visible sign to proclaim
the promise of the gospel for the forgiveness of sins and
eternal life. The sacramental sign seals this promise to
believers by grace and brings to them what is promised.
In baptism the sign is that of water; in the Lord's Supper, that of bread and wine.

The Study Catechism, 1998 (PCUSA)

Early on, Christians met in households. Church buildings
didn't start to appear for a couple of hundred years at least. More
than likely, especially in Corinth, church members met in the
home of a wealthy member who had enough room for everyone,
and they gathered on Sunday, the first day of the week. The well-
to-do members of the church typically brought food and shared
it, and the meal became the focus of their coming together.

People tended to come as soon as they left work. The first
day of the week — in ancient culture, anyway — was hardly a day
off, and so worship happened during the evening meal. Evi-
dently, according to Paul's description (11:17-22), what was happening in the Corinthian church was that those who arrived first,
the wealthy, began eating, and sometimes had too much to eat
and drink, while those who arrived late, usually the poor, were
humiliated because there was little or nothing left.

The Corinthians didn't share very well — not because they
had bad manners, but because they saw the meal as personal.
When they celebrated the sacrament, it was something that happened "between me and my Lord." Waiting for everyone to arrive
was something that didn't occur to them. Paul, however, encouraged them to think of the Lord's Supper in a new way, as a way of
practicing life in the Kingdom of God.

William Willimon, a Methodist minister, grew up in Greenville, South Carolina, and he remembers the civil rights struggle well. In one of his books, called *The Service of God*, he writes about the fight over who would be allowed to sit at a dime-store lunch counter. With tongue in cheek, Willimon writes that you have to "give the segregationists credit. They saw clearly that to share food with another person is to risk conversion. Something happens to people at a table." And then Willimon goes on to write about the political and ethical implications of this meal we share called the Lord's Supper.

Maybe you've never thought about the political and ethical implications of this sacrament. Maybe in all the years you've participated in it, you've never noticed that the meal has both vertical *and* horizontal dimensions. God meets us in the sacraments. That's true. But God also challenges us to think differently about our relationships with each other.

In the Presbyterian Church, the tradition in which I serve, the people who serve the meal are the leaders of the church — the pastors, the elders, and the deacons. The leaders take on the role of servants. We become kitchen help. And in doing so, we model a kind of leadership that is radically different from the kind you ordinarily see and hear about in the rest of culture.

Each time we celebrate the meal, we are reminding ourselves that we are different. The rules of the culture around us do not apply. We are called to be a new community, modeled and patterned after the example Jesus Christ, who was also a servant leader.

Here's another example. When we eat a meal together or sit down at the same table, we're making a kind of statement about our desire to get along. Most of us, like those segregationists in Greenville, would prefer not to eat with certain people, especially people who are different from us, people with whom we have differences of opinion. Eating at the lunch counter together is a lot like saying, "I accept you, even though you're not like me."

In the Lord's Supper, in our eating and drinking together, we demonstrate our oneness in Jesus Christ. Barriers disappear, if only for a few minutes. Our differences pale in importance. I feel it just about every time we celebrate the sacrament in my church. Because we talk about important and controversial subjects in the church, we sometimes disagree with each other. Conversations are occasionally difficult and strained. That happens in any family, and it happens in a church family. But during the sharing of the meal, something else happens. Sometimes I find myself breaking the bread and offering it to a person with whom I am in profound disagreement. But I become aware, as I offer the bread and say the words "the body of Christ broken for you," that something important is happening between us. The conflict, whatever it is, doesn't go away, but we have a reason for reconciliation.

May this your sacrament, Lord Jesus Christ,
bring life to us and pardon for our sins,
to us for whom you suffered your passion. . . .

You were laid in a new grave
to give us new grace in ages likewise anew.

The Apocryphal Acts of Thomas, 3rd century

---

*   *   *

Have you ever heard the phrase "means of grace"? That's an important one for Christians to know. I grew up hearing that I wasn't supposed to neglect the means of grace, though I really didn't understand fully what that meant. "Means of grace" is a way of referring to or thinking about the sacraments, and what the sacraments do is provide us with opportunities to develop the habits of the Christian life.

Sports physiologists would call it "muscle memory." If you perform a certain physical movement repeatedly, your muscles tend to remember it, to perform that action almost automatically. And so, as we return again and again to the Lord's table, to the source of our life together, it's as though our muscles — or in this case, our characters — learn what they need to know, perform an action that we hope will become almost second nature to us.

In fact, the hope is that coming to the Lord's table will eventually be as easy and as natural for us as coming to the breakfast table.

C. S. Lewis has a wonderful way of putting this. He says that worship itself — not just the sacraments — is like dancing. When we learn to dance, we concentrate on counting the steps. One, two, three. One, two, three. But the goal, Lewis writes, is to move beyond the counting to something that's effortless and enjoyable. As long as we're counting the steps, we're not really dancing. And the same is true of worship and the sacraments: the goal is to move beyond the "mechanics" of it, the counting of the steps, until it becomes natural.

And so, I suppose you could say that if everything we did in the Lord's Supper came naturally to us, there would be no reason to go over and over the lesson. But the truth is, none of this comes naturally to us. Being a servant leader doesn't come naturally to me. But I'm learning a little, week by week.

Seeing God in the mundane or common places of your life may not come naturally to you. But looking for God in the water of baptism and in the bread and wine of the Lord's Supper just may teach you to see God everywhere.

That bread we eat and the cup we share may look like ordinary stuff we buy at the grocery store. But the goal of the Christian life, the goal of our sanctification, is to start looking at the ordinary stuff — to say nothing of ordinary people — in some brand-new ways. And if we can recognize God in the Supper, then maybe, just maybe, we'll be able to recognize God in the faces of the people we meet each day.

Where in your life will you practice habits and behaviors like these if you don't practice them here? I don't know about you, but I need all the practice I can get.

QUESTIONS FOR FURTHER STUDY AND REFLECTION

1. Often when we celebrate the sacraments in worship, we feel passive, like spectators. What are we supposed to be doing when we celebrate the sacraments in church?

2. John Calvin wrote that God "condescends" to us in the sacraments. God isn't putting us down, so what did Calvin mean? Are there other ways that God "condescends" to us — in Calvin's sense of the word?

3. What does it mean that the sacraments are a "means of grace"? What are the other "means of grace" in your life?

Three Persons, One God

THE TRINITY

We believe in one God, the Father Almighty, Maker of heaven and earth, of all things visible and invisible; and in one Lord Jesus Christ, the only-begotten Son of God, begotten of the Father before all worlds, God of God, Light of Light, Very God of Very God, begotten, not made, being of one substance with the Father, by whom all things were made. . . . And we believe in the Holy Spirit, the Lord and Giver of life, who proceedeth from the Father and the Son.

Nicene Creed, 325

141

SUPPOSE I STOOD in the pulpit one Sunday and said, "Friends, the Trinity has always bothered me. I've never been able to understand it, although God knows I've tried. So I've decided to let you know today that I'm rejecting it once and for all."

If I were to say something like that, the people in my church would say, "Wow, he's really gone off the deep end. We can't have a minister here who doesn't believe in something as basic to the Christian faith as the Trinity."*

On the other hand, if I were to ask my congregation some Sunday to write down on a slip of paper why they thought the Trinity was so important, what difference the Trinity makes in their lives, I'm guessing that most of them couldn't do it. I'm guessing that most of them don't know why the doctrine of the Trinity is an essential doctrine of the Christian faith. Not because they aren't fine Christian people — they are — but because the doctrine of the Trinity itself is such a daunting concept to grasp. And most of us have long since given up the effort to do so.

Now, if that's the case, why would we insist that our ministers believe something that we ourselves couldn't explain to our neighbors or colleagues? If the Trinity is so important, so essential to our faith, shouldn't we be able to say something about its importance? My sense is that for the average Christian today, the Trinity has turned out to be more of an embarrassment than a joyful affirmation of the nature of God.

Maybe one reason that many Christians can't explain the importance of the Trinity is that the concept itself seems archaic. In a recent book called *God as Trinity*, theologian Ted Peters raises this very question. "Is the idea of the Trinity necessary dress for

---

*On October 27, 1553, Michael Servetus was publicly burned to death in Geneva for having denied the Trinity. The Reformer John Calvin often — and somewhat unfairly — receives blame for this execution. The truth is, Servetus was under threat of arrest nearly everywhere he went. And furthermore, just about anyone who denied the doctrine of the Trinity in sixteenth-century Europe would have faced a similar fate.

Christian faith," he asks, "or have we outgrown it? Should we discard it or keep it?" He argues that we should keep it, but to ask the question at all reveals something about our attitudes and feelings today. At some level, many of us are uncomfortable with the Trinity.

Author Dorothy Sayers believed that the average church member would describe the Trinity something like this: "The Father incomprehensible, the Son incomprehensible, and the whole thing incomprehensible. Something put in by theologians to make it more difficult — nothing to do with daily life or ethics."

Even for people who grasp the concept well enough and who could talk about it without embarrassment if they had to, the Trinity still seems unnecessarily complicated and abstract. One morning not long ago I taught an adult education class about the Trinity, and afterward a member of the church hurried over to me and said, "Why do we always make things so complicated around here? The only doctrine I need is, 'Jesus loves me, this I know, for the Bible tells me so.'"

Q. *Since there is but one God, why do you speak of three: Father, Son, and Holy Spirit?*

A. Because that is how
   God revealed himself in his Word:
   these three distinct persons
   are one, true, eternal God.

Lord's Day 8, Heidelberg Catechism, 1563

She had a point, and I quickly conceded it. I should have seen it coming. Whenever theological talk becomes separated from our faith or the issues that concern us most, our eyes tend to glaze over. We yearn for something simple, something that connects with our lives. I'm afraid my presentation that morning was so far removed from the faith of at least one person in the class that she started to reject the whole idea of theological reflection.

After our conversation, I found myself wishing that I could go back and teach the class again. I would have started with the church member's experience of God, and then I would have found a way to describe her experience in terms that made sense to her — *theological* terms. In spite of what she said, my suspicion is that "Jesus loves me" does not describe the full range of her religious experience — or the religious experience of most people. The God we meet in the Bible and the God we experience in our lives is far more complex and mysterious than we are able to describe. The doctrine of the Trinity can help us understand, organize, and describe our thinking about the God with whom we have to do.

*   *   *

You won't find the word *Trinity* in the Bible. Nor will you find the language of "three-in-one" or "three persons, one substance" in the Bible. It's not there. Nowhere does the Bible contain a doctrine of the Trinity. The doctrine we have today for the Trinity is the culmination of a long process spanning the first few centuries of the church.

Creation, history, Scripture, Jesus Christ, and Pentecost have always provided a wealth of information about the nature of God, and so the question for Christians has always been this: How do we make sense of all that information? How do we organize it in such a way that it holds together?

As early as the second century, the church's center of gravity shifted away from its origins in Palestine to the world of Greek thought. Christians worked hard to find a way of speaking about the Trinity that would make sense of what they observed about God, especially to the Greek mind. A number of Christian thinkers from this period (Justin Martyr, Irenaeus, Tertullian, and Origen) began to develop the basic outlines of trinitarian thought. In addition, a number of councils met, which had a great influence on the church and provided a common language about the Trinity. In particular, there was the Council of Nicea in 325, which was held at the invitation of emperor Constantine the Great. The decisive word to emerge from this council (suggested, interestingly enough, by the emperor himself) was *homoousios,* which means "of one substance." The Father and the Son, it was decided, were "of one substance." Consensus on that word represented an enormous breakthrough in the development of the doctrine of the Trinity, but the conversation was to continue for many years to come, with many more refinements.

In the end, here's what Christians came to think about the nature of God. First, they observed that God created the universe and then took care of it all. This person they called "God the Father." Next, they observed that this same God (*homoousios*) came to us in Jesus of Nazareth, having both divine and human natures. God was "up in heaven," but God was also "down here," alongside us or with us. This person they called "God the Son," the eternal Word or Logos who was with God from the beginning, at creation itself, and who was truly God. Finally, they observed that God came to us at Pentecost and could be found in us or among us as guide and friend. Jesus referred to this God who comes to us as the "Spirit of Truth" and the "Advocate." This person they called "God the Holy Spirit."

Above us. Alongside us. Within us. Three distinct persons, one substance, all together in perfect unity.

[God] who lives ever, and for ever reigns,
In mystic union of the Three in One,
Unbounded, bounding all.

Dante, *Paradise,* canto xiv, l. 28

Does the Trinity make sense? Yes. It's not as logical or rational as we perhaps would like it to be, but for Christian people the doctrine of the Trinity has provided a way to process all of the information we have about God. It's important for us to notice that the doctrine of the Trinity has its beginning as a *confession* of faith. We say it, or declare it, not because it's logical or rational, but because it describes the way we experience God.

The *doctrine* of the Trinity, then, is our attempt to describe or reflect on what we experience at the level of faith. The *doctrine* of the Trinity is a collection of images, words, and philosophical constructs that give expression to our faith. As such, this doctrine will always be inadequate; but it will always be our best attempt to say or express what we believe.

*   *   *

No discussion of the Trinity would be complete today without mentioning gender issues. All of our language about God is going to be limited, as we have seen in previous chapters, but nowhere is the problem as obvious or acute as it is when we talk about the Trinity.

One recent objection to the doctrine of the Trinity is that the traditional language is both sexist and idolatrous. In other words, the language of "Father" and "Son" casts God in the image of a male human being.

While this is an objection that ought to be taken seriously, it should be noted that the theologians who first crafted the doctrine of the Trinity did not necessarily think of God as male. It is true that they called God "Father" and they thought of Jesus as "Son," but they were well aware that maleness was not essential to any of the persons of the Trinity. They simply continued to use the language of the Bible. As theologian Shirley Guthrie puts it in his book *Christian Doctrine*, "They did not think of a great big Male up in the sky (with great big male 'parts')."

The creation story in Genesis makes clear that both men *and* women are created in the image of God. God transcends our gender differences. In fact, God's being is beyond anything we can conceive of or imagine (Isa. 55:8-9).

146

Batter my heart, three-person'd God; for you
As yet but knock, breathe, shine, and seek to mend;
That I may rise and stand, o'erthrow me, and bend
Your force to break, blow, burn, and make me new.

John Donne, "Holy Sonnets," 14

Some Christians, therefore, have suggested that it's time to abandon the language of "Father" and "Son." If it wasn't intended to be sexist back then, they say, it certainly is sexist today.

I've been in worship settings recently where the traditional language of "Father, Son, and Holy Spirit" has been replaced by "Creator, Redeemer, and Sustainer" — or similar formulas. And while I understand the desire to find language that better describes our understanding of God, we should probably recognize how difficult and even problematic such changes are. "Creator, Redeemer, Sustainer" language appears to solve one problem, but it immediately creates others. For example, all that we believe about God the Father cannot be contained in the word "Creator." The same can be said about "Redeemer" and "Sustainer." All that we believe about the Son is not contained in the word "Redeemer," and all that we believe about the Holy Spirit is not contained in the word "Sustainer." Those words describe specific tasks ascribed to those persons, but we believe that those persons are far more and accomplish far more than those words suggest.

Moreover, phrases like "Creator, Redeemer, and Sustainer" do not adequately capture the kind of relationship that we believe exists among the members of the Trinity. "Father" and "Son" are personal and imply a kind of intimacy that "Creator" and "Redeemer" simply do not. When we finally settle on appropriate language for the persons of the Trinity — if we ever do — that language must suggest an inner life of warmth, trust, and intimacy which, as we will see later in this chapter, have come to be considered essential characteristics of the Trinity.

One more small wrinkle. The gender of the Hebrew word for "Spirit" (*ruach*), which can also mean "wind" or "breath," is feminine. Some theologians believe this may have implications for the Trinity. They speculate, for example, that the Holy Spirit may provide a gender balance to the Trinity. As with many trinitarian discussions, however, there doesn't seem to be much consensus about what the gender of "Spirit" might mean. For what it's worth, the gender of the Greek word for "Spirit" is neuter, while the gender of the Latin word is masculine. Perhaps it's enough to say, as theologian Shirley Guthrie has, that the Holy Spirit is personal, not some*thing* but some*one*.

*   *   *

When people think about the Trinity today, it's not only gender issues that come to mind. People are talking about hierarchical issues too.

Somehow, in the history of thinking about the Trinity, many if not most people in the West have adopted the visual image of a triangle. The Father is situated at the top, while the Son and Holy Spirit are at the bottom. In this view, the Father is clearly pre-eminent, the "Almighty," while the Son and the Holy Spirit are seen as lesser beings. Exalted, perhaps, but something less than the Father. Instead of suggesting that perfect equality and mutuality exist among the members of the Trinity, this particular image has fostered the idea that there's a hierarchy embedded in the very structure of the Godhead.

Early in the history of the church, theologians and other leaders worked to eradicate a number of errors in trinitarian thinking (sometimes called "heresies"), and among them was an error referred to as "subordinationism," which grew out of this hierarchical model. In spite of the church's best efforts, though, the distortion has persisted, and the result is that this hierarchical model has found its way into some of our most basic human relationships — individual, familial, and social. What has happened, according to those who raise this issue, is that hierarchical thinking, seemingly supported by the doctrine of the Trinity, has distorted the way we are with each other. Issues of power and authority, for example, get in the way of the healthy relationships God wants for us.

The tragedy in all of this is that the Trinity appears to point us to something else entirely. In our effort to think of God as one, we have somehow missed the sense in which the Trinity is also a society of persons, a society characterized by mutual love. Theologians sometimes call this the "social Trinity." In *Faith Seeking Understanding*, theologian Daniel Migliore writes that "the unity of God is not undifferentiated, dead unity. The Trinity is essentially a *koinonia* of persons in love."

Question 17. What does our creation in God's image reflect about God's reality?
Our being created in and for relationship is a reflection of the Holy Trinity. In the mystery of the one God, the three divine persons — Father, Son, and Holy Spirit — live in, with and for one another eternally in perfect love and freedom.

The Study Catechism, 1998 (PCUSA)

Speculation about the inner mystery of God might seem like a waste of time, if it weren't for the implications for our own lives. Is it possible that the inner life of God has something to tell us about the way we are with each other?

In Eastern Orthodoxy, the circle — not the triangle — has always been the dominant mental image for the Trinity. In the religious art or icons of the Orthodox Church, Father, Son, and Holy Spirit are often pictured sitting together around a table and sharing a meal. John of Damascus, a Greek theologian of the eighth century, developed the concept of *perichoresis* (literally, "dancing around"). In this view, Father, Son, and Holy Spirit are like danc-

149

ers who hold hands and dance around together, sharing a harmonious and joyful life.

Think of the implications of this image for our lives today. In this sort of union, there is no above and below, no first, second, and third in importance, no ruling and controlling (or being ruled and controlled), no question of who is in charge. Instead, Father, Son, and Holy Spirit are related — each free *for* the others, not *from* the others. The persons of the Trinity do not exist in absolute autonomy, as self-enclosed subjects having no relationship with each other. Instead, the persons of the Trinity exist in community. They are interdependent. They give and receive love. They are differentiated by function, not by place of importance.

In recent theological conversation, all of these issues have been debated and explored in considerable detail. Some theologians have constructed Christian ethics based on these trinitarian insights. The Trinity continues to be an intensely debated topic, as it was in the early days of the church, and no one is claiming to have spoken the last word. What's exciting is that as we come to a better understanding of God, we also come to a better understanding of ourselves.

If the description here of a social Trinity is indeed a glimpse into the inner life or nature of God, what are the implications for our own lives together — in marriage, family, and community life? Do we need to rethink some of those relationships?

Above us, alongside us, within us. Tell me, is this how you experience God?

It's possible, if you're like the church member I mentioned at the beginning of this chapter, that "Jesus loves me, this I know" seems like an adequate statement of faith to you. But Christian tradition tells us that there is more to God than that. The God we worship, the God who loves us, is far larger than we sometimes know, more mysterious and certainly more complex.

Calling God "Father, Son, and Holy Spirit" is the best way we know — the best way Christians down through the centuries have known — to describe God fully and completely.

How would you describe the God you see in creation, read about in the Bible, and experience in your life?

QUESTIONS FOR FURTHER STUDY AND REFLECTION

1. Why is a doctrine like the Trinity even necessary? What does it explain?

2. The Greek-speaking Eastern churches and the Latin-speaking Western churches went in slightly different directions, with different emphases. What can Western Christians learn from the Eastern tradition? Is there something Eastern Christians could learn from the West?

3. Some Christians have found the baptismal formula "Father, Son, and Holy Spirit" problematic because of its gender references. Can you think of other language that adequately describes the triune God?

Last Things

ESCHATOLOGY

When I was six months old, I nearly died. All wrong for an infant to be caught up in the last things. . . . But the struggle that took place in my infant body and still-forming, preverbal intelligence was between life and death, and I am convinced that a sense of something vast, something yet to come, took hold in my unconscious and remains there still. The word "eschatology" no longer seems otherworldly to me, or even focused exclusively on future events. It seems more in tune with quantum physics and its sense of time as fluid. I have to regard the word as life-affirming in ways far more subtle than any dictionary definition could convey.

Kathleen Norris, *Amazing Grace:*
A Vocabulary of Faith

D O YOU EVER find yourself wondering where all of this is going? Life, that is. Do you ever wonder what's going to become of
you? And what about your children or your grandchildren? What
will become of them?

My ninety-six-year-old grandmother, who died recently,
used to shake her head in disbelief when she thought about the
world that my children are entering. It's so vastly different from
the world she entered at their age. My grandmother thought
about the future a lot. In fact, in the last years of her life, it was
the subject she thought about most.

Where *is* all of this going?

Our faith has answers to those questions. But my guess is
that, as with those other subjects we've explored, we're probably
not able to say with much confidence what Christians believe
about the future. Many Christians today probably don't know exactly what our tradition teaches about the "Last Things," as they're
sometimes called, and I think that's too bad, because I think
people of faith should be able to say what they believe — not just
about today but about tomorrow. We should know where "all of
this" is going. Or at least we should have a pretty good idea.

*   *   *

In 1970 a man named Hal Lindsey published a book called *The
Late Great Planet Earth*. In the years since then, this book has become one of the best-selling books in history.

What Hal Lindsey did was look at the Bible, especially books
such as Daniel and Revelation, and then look at history, especially recent history. And finally, in a very popular and readable
way, he showed how all of it fits together, how the Bible predicts
the course of history and current events. Clearly, as he saw it, we
are living in "the last times" — which is another way that people
sometimes refer to this subject. The return of Christ, Lindsey de-
clared, is imminent. All signs point to the end of history as we
know it.

Something about this book and its point of view captured the attention of many American Christians. What Hal Lindsey wrote seemed to fit with what many people, many *Christian* people, saw on the front page of their newspapers. The Middle East was in turmoil. The former Soviet Union appeared ready to use its enormous power. "Could it be?" millions of people wondered. "Could we actually be near the end of history as we know it?"

Of course, Hal Lindsey wasn't the first person to write a book like this, but he did it better than most. Maybe his timing was just right too. But there was really nothing new about his point of view. Hal Lindsey is part of a long line of Christian people who have looked hard for signs of the end.

There will be signs in the sun, the moon, and the stars, and on the earth distress among nations confused by the roaring of the sea and the waves. People will faint from fear and foreboding of what is coming upon the world, for the powers of the heavens will be shaken. Then they will see "the Son of Man coming in a cloud" with power and great glory. Now when these things begin to take place, stand up and raise your heads, because your redemption is drawing near.

Luke 21:25-28

In 1909, C. I. Scofield, a lawyer by training, published the Scofield Reference Bible, which, in supplemental notes, charts, and diagrams, divided history into a series of dispensations (hence the term "dispensationalism," which is one school of thought about the Last Things). According to Scofield's calculations, twentieth-century Christians were clearly living in the last times, awaiting only the final return of Christ, the rapture, and the thousand-year reign of Christ, as predicted by the Bible. Interestingly enough, the Scofield Bible was reissued in 1967, just a few years before Lindsey's book, perhaps indicating a resurgence of popular interest in where history was moving.

Shirley Guthrie, one of the theologians in my own Reformed tradition, calls these Christians — Scofield, Lindsey, and others like them — "historical pessimists." Their reading of history, he says, is essentially pessimistic. Things are going from bad to worse, as they see it. Cataclysmic, end-of-the-world events will continue to occur, and with greater frequency. Only Christ's return will put everything right again. The sooner, the better. "Come, Lord Jesus" is their fervent prayer.

Christians, as you can probably guess, aren't the only people who qualify as "historical pessimists." Many writers and thinkers in the last century have pointed, in one way or another, to the decline of morality, the erosion of civility, and the disintegration of the social order. John Updike, one of the most important novelists of the last half-century, has published a book called *Toward the End of Time*. The story is set in the future, about three hundred years from now. Nuclear war has broken out. Millions and millions of people have been killed. Life in the future, at least as Updike describes it, is both grim and ugly.

This point of view has taken root in our world, I'm afraid, and for many of us it's depressing. It's certainly not what we would call life-affirming. Historical pessimists get our attention largely because they appeal to our fears. After all, what if they're right? Things *are* bad today, aren't they? And they seem to be getting worse instead of better. It's easy to find yourself caught up in predictions of imminent catastrophe.

Predictions of global chaos and widespread disasters are also associated with the coming millennium. My sense is that people who are excessivly worried about the "Y2K phenomenon" are also historical pessimists.

But historical pessimism isn't the only point of view out there. Guthrie says we also have "historical optimists" among us. And historical optimists believe that things are actually getting better and better — or that they could be better than they are through human effort. We have the tools, these people say, to eliminate poverty. We have the capacity to end hunger. We know what it takes for races and ethnic groups to live together in harmony. Now all we have to do is *do* it.

Historical optimism isn't the traditional Christian view, but along the way many Christians, including many Presbyterians, have tended to be historical optimists. Presbyterians are sometimes known for having established schools and colleges all over the American frontier. The thinking was that, if we taught people how to read and write, if we gave them the gift of education, then the Kingdom of God would be that much closer. Many saw education as one important engine to help prepare the way for the Kingdom.

Presbyterians have always been involved in government too — often in numbers disproportionate to the actual size of the Presbyterian church. I don't think it's true any longer, but there was a time not very many years ago when there were more Presbyterians in Congress than there were members of any other religious group. Why? Well, we Presbyterians believed that we could make the world a better place. We thought of ourselves as partners in God's plan for the future.

How about "the Great Society"? In the 1960s the Great Society actually seemed to be within our reach, though today the whole notion seems like a terribly misguided idea. All of those government programs designed to lift people out of poverty? What were we thinking? Now people have come to think of it derisively as "the welfare state," but back then many American people actually thought that anything was possible.

How about *Star Trek* — the original television series and all of its subsequent incarnations? Even the entertainment industry seems to have a point of view on the future. And really, who isn't attracted to a vision of the future where hunger and racism have been overcome, where people have learned to cooperate and live together in peace, and where the most important mission in life is to "explore strange new worlds"? The continuing commercial success of *Star Trek* tells me that many, many people want to believe the best about our future.

What *does* the future hold for us? Should we be optimistic about it — or not? What exactly is God's plan for us and our world?

"And remember, I am with you always, to the end of the age."

Matthew 28:20

---

*   *   *

I think it's important to recognize that many Christians — and Reformed Christians in particular — have never been either historical pessimists or historical optimists. I think we've been optimistic about the future, but only because we believe God is in control, not necessarily because the world itself is getting better and better. I'm not sure, you see, that it is.

Let me sketch out for you, as briefly as I can, what my own branch of the Christian tradition has always said about this particular subject — though, as I've suggested, it's important to remember that this topic has been hotly debated by Christians in recent years. Theologians like Jürgen Moltmann have written extensively about the future, introducing new and perhaps even exciting ways for the Christian to think not just about the future but about the nature of time itself. Some of these ideas will no doubt find their way eventually into mainstream Christian thinking, but in this discussion I want to say as simply as I can where Christians have been, not where they might be going.

When I think about the future in theological terms, at least one biblical reference comes to mind — Jesus' words as recorded in Luke's Gospel, the ones about his coming again on the clouds of heaven.

Christians — especially Reformed Christians, as I suggested in an earlier chapter — take a high view of Scripture. We are people of the Word. But we believe that, to be understood, Scripture requires our careful interpretation. So when the Bible says, for example, that Jesus will come again "on the clouds of heaven," how do we read that? In a literal way? Would those be the clouds over Chicago? Or the clouds over Jerusalem? Or the clouds over your hometown?

Another biblical reference comes to mind — from Paul's first letter to the Thessalonians. This one says that there will be a trumpet blast at the end of history. So my question is, What kind of trumpet would that be? One that every person on the planet would be able to hear, a God-sized trumpet?

As we read verses like these that describe the end of time, we need to remember that the language is often going to be an approximation. The words of Scripture are describing something that almost certainly is beyond the range of human experience as well as beyond the scope of human language. Jesus himself said that he didn't know important details about the end, important details like the day and the time (Mark 13:32), but then he went ahead and used word pictures so that we would have some sense of what he was trying to explain.

The context of First Thessalonians (especially 4:13–5:11) tells us that some people were very concerned about the end. They expected Christ's return to be imminent, and they were concerned about those who had already died. Would they get to see Christ too? The Apostle Paul answered their questions in a compassionate, almost tender way. He said, "I don't want you to be uninformed about this, brothers and sisters." Then he explained how — dead or alive — we will all at some point be together with God. The intent certainly seemed to be to calm our fears, to set our minds at rest, especially concerning those who have already died. Paul even said, "Encourage each other with these words."

And so, to read these verses, especially the ones about a rapture (believers being taken up into the clouds to be with Christ), and then to use them to warn or threaten others about the future would, I think, be a serious misinterpretation of the biblical material. And yet that's precisely how these verses often seem to be

> For the Lord himself, with a cry of command, with the archangel's call and with the sound of God's trumpet, will descend from heaven, and the dead in Christ will rise first. Then we who are alive, who are left, will be caught up in the clouds together with them to meet the Lord in the air; and so we will be with the Lord forever. Therefore encourage one another with these words.
>
> 1 Thessalonians 4:16-18

used by otherwise well-meaning interpreters of Scripture.* In some Christian traditions, references to the Last Things (eschatology) have been used to get the attention of people who are living — how shall I put it? — casual lives. No matter how noble or righteous the intent, the effect has been to frighten people into listening to the Christian message.

Occasionally in my community, where there are more historical pessimists per capita than any other community I have ever lived in, I'll see a bumper sticker with the words "In case of rapture, this car will be without a driver." And when I do, I can almost guarantee that the driver is not a person from my own theological tradition.

The sense I get from the Bible is that Paul wants to relieve us of our anxieties about the future, not compound them.

*   *   *

Let me tell you something else about my own branch of the Christian tradition. (This may be one reason why I don't remember hearing many sermons about eternity when I was growing

---

*In a recent series of novels by Tim La Haye, the rapture has become the setting for some interesting and, I would say, harrowing experiences for Christians.

up.) In my tradition, Christians figure that the future is in God's hands, and so it's a waste of time to worry about it. God has so much more in mind for us than speculating about a future we can't quite see from here.

Except for the biblical references I've given already — and obviously the books of Daniel in the Old Testament and Revelation in the New Testament — the Bible doesn't have all that much to say about the end. Most biblical writers didn't speculate about the end very much because they lived in joyful and confident anticipation of it. That's important for us to see. In a way it's a model of living for us.

John Calvin, in many ways the architect of our theological tradition, has a few words of caution for us too. He wrote that "it's foolish and rash to inquire concerning unknown matters more deeply than God wants us to know." I think that's exactly right. But he wasn't alone in wanting to warn us. Reinhold Niebuhr put it this way: "It is unwise for Christians to claim any knowledge of either the furniture of heaven or the temperature of hell; or to be too certain about any details of the kingdom of God in which history is consummated." I like that one too.

So what do people in our tradition do if they don't want to be "foolish and rash" or "unwise"? They live their lives in the here and now. If the Bible doesn't say much about tomorrow, it sure has a lot of detail about today. You and I have our hands full right now living the lives that God calls us to. The future is God's responsibility; how we live today is ours.

*   *   *

Let me offer one last insight. One theologian I know writes, "If you want to know how God will act in the future, all you have to do is notice how God has acted in the past."

There are well-meaning Christians, as I've mentioned, who spend their time scouring the Old Testament prophecies and looking for tiny clues about the end of time. And to those well-meaning but misguided people, we might want to say, "You're making it way too hard. We have all the evidence we need right now to know what God will do in the future."

God's plan to restore creation and put things right was set in motion back in the early chapters of Genesis. God has a track record that goes back that far. Then, of course, there was the birth of Jesus in Bethlehem nearly two thousand years ago. Quite a lot occurred in between too. So if you know anything about God's track record, then you can be confident that God will always act out of love for his creation.

Some people — though not, I've noticed, as many as in previous generations — carry around a mental image of a terrible Last Judgment. Although this event is described with relatively few details in the Bible, Michelangelo made the Last Judgment disturbingly vivid with his famous painting in the Sistine Chapel. Wherever our image of the judgment comes from, I have known people who have tortured themselves with fear over what this final event would be like — either for themselves or for those they loved. I was in a Bible study not long ago with a man who talked openly about his fear of the final judgment. He just couldn't be sure, he said with obvious emotion, how God would deal with him.

Fix our steps, O Lord, that we may not stagger at the uneven motions of the world, but steadily go on to our glorious home, neither censuring our journey by the weather we meet with, nor turning out of the way by anything that befalls us. . . . Through Jesus Christ our Lord.

John Wesley,
"This Transitory Life"

But here again, God has a track record that ought to relieve our anxieties. The one who Scripture says will sit as judge is none other than Jesus Christ, and he is the one who died on the cross for us — to remove God's judgment from us.

Is there anything to fear about that? I don't think so. I know what I deserve, of course, but the good news is that God won't deal with me on that basis. The God I read about in both the Old and New Testaments is a God who deals with us on the basis of grace. That's my only hope. So that's the hope with which I live my life. The Heidelberg Catechism says that we can face the final judgment, whatever it looks like, with our heads held high. God's Spirit will enable us to "firmly resist our enemies until we finally win the complete victory."

What does the future hold for you and me? What will the end look like? I don't know for sure, and neither does anyone else. The specifics aren't as clear as some Christians would like to think. But this much we do know: the future is in God's hands. Which is good news.

But there's more: you and I are called to be accountable for the way we live our lives today. And that's the challenge that should occupy whatever time we have left.

QUESTIONS FOR FURTHER STUDY AND REFLECTION

1. Many Christians are fascinated with talk about the "Last Things." Novels about life after the rapture, for example, are best-sellers. Other Christians, by contrast, seem unconcerned about the future. They're trying to make life better right now. Where are you? How do we make up our minds about an issue like this?

2. "Biblical language about the future is metaphorical or symbolic." Do you agree with this statement?

3. I like the advice that goes like this: "If you want to know what God will do in the future, look at what God has done in the past." What does God's track record in the past tell you about what God will do in the future?

The Word Made Flesh

THE INCARNATION

The one thoroughly laid down and safe way to avoid all going wide of the truth is the doctrine of the Incarnation — that one and the same person is God and man; as God, the end of our going; as man, the way we are to go.

St. Augustine, The City of God

WHAT DOES IT MEAN that "the Word became flesh and lived among us"?

My own preference is to reflect on this question in July — or at least not in the days and weeks leading up to Christmas. For me, the holiday tends to get in the way, and I too easily forget what the season commemorates. Still, the question is an important one. What *is* Christmas about? What *does* it mean that the "the Word became flesh"?

*   *   *

One year, a few days before Christmas, I was feeling down. I could point to all of the usual reasons, too — stress of ministry, seasonal obligations, the long hours of darkness. I remember driving along Roosevelt Road, a major east-west artery in the Chicago area, and noticing a sign outside an office building with these words: "There's a reason for the season."

I surprised myself with my glum response. "I sure hope so," I remember thinking, "because there's got to be a good reason for going through all of this."

The question then and now is, "What in the world is it?"

*   *   *

As often as Christians have heard the story, as often as we've been to the Sunday school Christmas pageants, as often as we've observed the nativity scenes that decorate our homes and lawns at Christmas, I wonder how many of us can really say what the Incarnation is about.

Christmas celebrates a mystery, a *holy* mystery, one that's as difficult to describe as any I've mentioned so far: *God somehow became a human being without ceasing to be God.* God came to us — not in a way that drew much attention to itself, but in the flesh, in the person of Jesus of Nazareth.

Let me point out something that's been helpful to my own

understanding of the Christmas story, a truth that helps to keep Christmas in perspective for me. During Jesus' ministry, no one in the Gospel accounts came to believe in him because of the circumstances of his birth — except perhaps for his mother and the shepherds, though even *that's* not entirely clear. No one, as far as we know, heard the story of Jesus' birth and then said, "Oh, that's marvelous. I simply must know more about him."

Only after people heard Jesus speak, only after people watched him in action and came to know him, did they begin to ask questions. Once, when Jesus taught in his hometown synagogue (Matt. 13:54-58), the people were so startled by what he said — and how he said it — that they started talking among themselves about his origins: "Isn't this the carpenter's son?" they asked. "Isn't Mary his mother? Don't we know his brothers and sisters?"

Question 22. How did Christ, being the Son of God, become man?
Christ, the Son of God, became man by taking to himself a true body and a reasonable soul, being conceived by the power of the Holy Spirit, in the womb of the Virgin Mary, and born of her, yet without sin.

Westminster Shorter Catechism, 1647

In nearly every case, the question of Jesus' origins became important only later — after people had been moved by his words. (Occasionally when people were annoyed by something Jesus said, they brought up the circumstances of his birth as a way to discredit or belittle him.) Naturally *we* read the Gospels from beginning to end. *We* start with the stories of his birth and end with the stories of his death and resurrection. But for the people who knew him first, it was the other way around. First they noticed something remarkable about him and what he said, and only then did they begin to ask questions about the circumstances of his birth. Some scholars have even suggested that the birth stories in Matthew and Luke were added at a later point in the development of those two Gospels — to satisfy the natural curiosity that later believers had.

Interestingly, the Apostle Paul makes almost no mention whatsoever of the circumstances surrounding Jesus' birth. My guess is that if Paul had known about those circumstances or if he had thought they might have some value for his evangelistic work, he would have written about them. But he didn't, and sometimes what isn't said is just as important as what is.

In many ways we're not so different from those early Christians. The Christmas story doesn't really become important for us either until we've heard something about Jesus' life and ministry. It's then that we're moved to ask, "Where did *he* come from? How is it that he came to be with us? Isn't this the son of Joseph, the carpenter?"

*   *   *

One observation about Jesus' virgin birth.

Theologians don't defend the virgin birth because it proves Jesus' divinity. It doesn't. Christians today don't believe Jesus was Emmanuel or "God with us" because he was born of a virgin. The virgin birth doesn't *prove* anything, except perhaps that his birth was a medical anomaly. We say the words of the Apostles' Creed ("conceived by the Holy Spirit, born of the Virgin Mary") to remind ourselves that Jesus came to us from God and that he came to life as we all did — namely, by being born. We certainly don't mean to imply that Jesus is a strange, mythological creature, half-God and half-man.

The only reason people became interested in the nature of his conception — as with other details of his birth — is that they first believed there was something remarkable about him when he was an adult. Jesus' authority arose from who he was and what he said and did. His authority was not conferred on him by the unusual circumstances of his birth.

Why bother to make this point?

My concern here is to describe the way we come to faith, the means by which we say we believe. We don't believe in Jesus' teachings because of his unique birth; we believe in his teachings because they're true. They merit our attention and belief in and of themselves. We find ourselves convicted and convinced by his words. Sometimes it's as though he is speaking directly to us, and as he does so, our lives are changed. Then and only then do we become interested in the person behind the words.

At that point we find ourselves saying, along with faithful people of all times, "Who *is* this?" And in response to the question, our statement of faith becomes "This is Jesus, who was 'conceived by the Holy Spirit, born of the Virgin Mary.'"

The same sort of thing happened at the end of Jesus' life. When the Roman soldier who crucified Jesus realized that this man was no ordinary criminal, he suddenly uttered a statement of faith: "Truly this was the Son of God."

*   *   *

Here's a helpful way to understand the mystery of the Incarnation: At Christmas, then and now, God and human beings appear to travel in opposite directions.

He was made what we are that He might make us what He is Himself.

Irenaeus, *Against Heresies*

When you and I get ready for Christmas, we dress up. Even if we're not in an especially festive mood, we do it because we yearn to be happier than we are. It's a longing that often goes with the time of year. To borrow the words of the song, we "deck the halls" and "don . . . our gay apparel." And my sense is that we look good at Christmas — or at least we try our best. I don't think my home ever looks quite as cozy and inviting as it does just before Christmas. The city of Wheaton too. I love to drive home from church through downtown Wheaton late at night after a long, tedious meeting. The lights and decorations point to something special and wonderful. When I look at them, I sometimes — though not always! — find my hope restored.

But there's more. At Christmastime I also love to stand at the door of the church and greet people after worship. Everyone comes to church dressed in clothes they apparently keep at the back of the drawer and closet. One time I shook hands with a man who was wearing a candy-cane tie and red socks with tiny green bells that actually made noise when he walked. He looked as though he was going to a party — which in a way he was. Before that, I hadn't known him to be an especially playful person. But there he was, and to me his dress was a sign that *something* was happening in the world.

Now, what's important to notice is that, while we're dressing up, while we're trying to put ourselves in what we call the holiday spirit, God is moving in another direction entirely. Spiritually, we seem to be reaching or grasping for something, while God is divesting, letting go, dressing down. To me this is the wonderful irony of the season. Theologian Mary Ellen Ashcroft has described it this way: "To get ready for Christmas, God undressed." That sentence got my attention when I first read it, which was undoubtedly the reason she wrote it that way, and I wanted to hear more.

This is how she puts it: "God stripped off his finery and appeared — how embarrassing — naked on the day he was born. God rips off medals of rank, puts aside titles, honors, and talents, appears in his birthday suit. *Veiled in flesh the Godhead see; hail the incarnate deity.*"

For some Christians, this may be an altogether new way of thinking about Christmas. The Christmas story is about a God who came to us in a disturbingly human way. At Christmas the creator of the universe was downwardly mobile, though it's often difficult for us to appreciate exactly how much God gave up for us — or the distance God had to travel to be one of us.

In Colossians (1:15-20), some of the references to Jesus' exalted status may be lost on us. Their full meaning may not be immediately clear. And yet, the language there — in phrases like "the image of the invisible God" — is the language kings in the ancient world appropriated for themselves. The Apostle Paul borrows that language to make the contrast clear. "Here's what God gave up," he seems to say, "to become one of us."

*   *   *

People in the ancient world — Greeks and Romans — laughed at the idea of a god become flesh. It was preposterous from their point of view, so different from anything that had ever been proposed before. Of course, a god might have a fling once in a while with a mortal woman, but then that god always disappeared again into the heavenly realms. It was almost as though there was an understanding that gods and human beings would keep their distance from each other. The way it worked for ancient people was that there was a great big God up there and little, finite human beings down here.

In a way, our expectations haven't changed all that much. Isn't there something just a little unsettling or even scary about a God who decides to come into the world crying and needing to hear the sound of his mother's voice and desperately wanting to nurse? I held my own daughters just moments after they were born, and much as I loved that experience and still cherish it today, there is something just a little bothersome about the thought that God came into the world the same way. Utterly helpless and uncomprehending. To me it's as disturbing as it is beautiful.

Even the devil, according to the Gospel story, knew that there was something unsettling about this picture, and so when Jesus as a young adult went into the wilderness, the story says

171

> God could, had He pleased, have been incarnate in a man of iron nerves, the Stoic sort who lets no sigh escape him. Of His great humility He chose to be incarnate in a man of delicate sensibilities who wept at the grave of Lazarus and sweated blood in Gethsemane.
>
> C. S. Lewis, *Letters of C. S. Lewis*

that the devil approached him and offered him the opportunity to make something of himself. The story is a familiar one. There were three temptations, but the theme was essentially the same in all of them: "Jesus, you ought to be more . . . well, godly. You ought to look and act the part. You should be moving in better circles than you are. Bad enough that you weren't born somewhat better. Here's your chance to change all that."

But Jesus rejected the suggestion. His mission was not to become great but to become small. His strategy, if you can call it that, wasn't to work from a position of strength; his strategy was to be weak and suffer.

God knew, better than we ever will, that the best way to put things right in the world, the best way to restore creation to what it was intended to be, wasn't to overpower it. God knew that the best and perhaps the only solution was to love the world and to love the people in it. Not just to talk about love, either, but to demonstrate it, to make it real, to give it flesh and blood.

*   *   *

In traditional Christian doctrine about Jesus, you'll typically find the language of "humiliation" and "exaltation." Jesus' birth, it is said, was the beginning of his humiliation. What's important for us to see, though, is that his birth was also the beginning, in a way, of *our* exaltation.

Here's why I believe the Incarnation is such good news for us: In the Incarnation, all of humanity — humanity in all its ugliness, with all its limitations — was lifted up. God let us know once again what God always intended — that to be a human being is good. Or can be. Life itself can be good, is *supposed* to be good. It's possible to live a good and fully authentic life. Existence isn't something that we need to escape; because it's good, existence can be enjoyed, just as Jesus himself thoroughly enjoyed the good times. By "becoming flesh and living among us," Jesus took up our cause; in fact, he made our cause *God's* cause. As one theologian puts it, "Now, with the birth of Jesus, if you were against human beings, any of them, you were against God." With the Incarnation, God made it absolutely clear whose side he was on.

O God, who looked on us when we had fallen down into death, and resolved to redeem us by the Advent of your only begotten Son; grant . . . that those who confess his glorious Incarnation may also be admitted to the fellowship of their Redeemer, through the same Jesus Christ our Lord.

St. Ambrose

Everything God intended for human beings was present in Jesus, and it was almost as though God was saying, "Look at this man. If you want to know what it means to be a genuine and authentic human being, to stand for what's right in the world, look at Jesus. And if you want to know who God is and what God is doing in the world, then look at Jesus too. It's all there in this one person."

*   *   *

That's why I think the Incarnation isn't only good news — it's also scary news. If God undressed, you see, then we might have to join him. We might have to let go of some things — like our own need to be strong and powerful and in control. We might have to become more like him. To satisfy the hunger inside us, the hunger I mentioned at the beginning of this book, the *God* hunger that drives us more than most of us admit, we may have to let a lot of things go. In the end, that's the only way to open ourselves to the God who has come an unimaginable distance to meet us.

All of the basic Christian doctrine I've described in this book isn't going to mean much — it's going to remain an intellectual exercise — if we don't open ourselves to the God who stands behind it all. Even the doctrine of the Incarnation is going to remain just that — a doctrine — unless we somehow allow him to be born in us, to come alive inside us.

John's Gospel calls Jesus a "light shining in the darkness." The darkness, it says, did not overcome that light. Still, the world did not know him, and his own people did not accept him. But, the story continues, to all who received him he gave power, power to become children of God.

I think that's the reason for the season, don't you? More than anything else, I want to be a child of God. Better yet, I want to believe what I have always been taught — that I am *already* a child of God.

QUESTIONS FOR FURTHER STUDY AND REFLECTION

1. The New Testament is relatively silent about the virgin birth. The Apostle Paul wrote in Galatians 4:4 that Jesus was "born of a woman," but made no other references to this teaching. Why is the virgin birth of Jesus important?

2. In what sense is Jesus' humiliation the beginning of our exaltation?

3. Was it important that Jesus actually became a human being? Wouldn't it have been enough if he simply appeared to be human?

Bibliography

(In addition to most of the works I've cited in the text, I've included a few other titles here that fall under the "suggested reading" category.)

Allen, Diogenes. *The Reasonableness of Faith: A Philosophical Essay on the Grounds for Religious Belief.* Washington-Cleveland: Corpus Publications, 1968.

Bartow, Charles L. *God's Human Speech: A Practical Theology of Proclamation.* Grand Rapids: William B. Eerdmans, 1997.

Behe, Michael. *Darwin's Black Box: The Biochemical Challenge to Evolution.* New York: Free Press, 1996.

Berger, Peter L. *A Rumor of Angels: Modern Society and the Rediscovery of the Supernatural.* Garden City, N.Y.: Doubleday-Anchor, 1970.

Bruner, Frederick Dale. *A Theology of the Holy Spirit: The Pentecostal Experience and the New Testament Witness.* Grand Rapids: William B. Eerdmans, 1970.

Buchanan, John M. *Being Church, Becoming Community.* Louisville: Westminster John Knox, 1996.

Callahan, Kennon. *Effective Church Leadership: Building on the Twelve Keys.* San Francisco: Harper & Row, 1990.

Calvin, John. *Institutes*. Grand Rapids: William B. Eerdmans, 1986.

Coles, Robert. *The Spiritual Life of Children*. Boston: Houghton Mifflin, 1990.

Crossan, John Dominic. *Jesus: A Revolutionary Biography*. San Francisco: HarperSan Francisco, 1994.

Dillard, Annie. *Pilgrim at Tinker Creek*. New York: Bantam Books, 1975.

Evans, C. Stephen. *Why Believe? Reason and Mystery as Pointers to God*. Grand Rapids: William B. Eerdmans, 1996.

Fackre, Gabriel. *The Doctrine of Revelation: A Narrative Interpretation*. Grand Rapids: William B. Eerdmans, 1997.

Feenstra, Ronald J., and Cornelius Plantinga Jr. *Trinity, Incarnation, and Atonement: Philosophical and Theological Essays*. Notre Dame: University of Notre Dame Press, 1989.

Gomes, Peter. *The Good Book: Reading the Bible with Mind and Heart*. New York: William Morrow, 1996.

Guthrie, Shirley C. *Christian Doctrine*. Louisville: Westminster John Knox, 1994.

Hauerwas, Stanley, and William H. Willimon. *Resident Aliens: Life in the Christian Colony*. Nashville: Abingdon, 1990.

McCullough, Donald W. *The Trivialization of God: The Dangerous Illusion of a Manageable Deity*. Colorado Springs: NavPress, 1995.

Migliore, Daniel L. *Faith Seeking Understanding: An Introduction to Christian Theology*. Grand Rapids: William B. Eerdmans, 1991.

Peters, Ted. *God as Trinity*. Louisville: Westminster John Knox, 1993.

Peterson, Eugene. *Leap over a Wall: Earthy Spirituality for Everyday Christians*. San Francisco: HarperCollins, 1997.

————. *Working the Angles: The Shape of Pastoral Integrity*. Grand Rapids: William B. Eerdmans, 1993.

Plantinga, Cornelius Jr. *Not the Way It's Supposed to Be: A Breviary of Sin*. Grand Rapids: William B. Eerdmans, 1996.

Purdy, John C. *God with a Human Face*. Louisville: Westminster John Knox, 1993.

176

Sayers, Dorothy. *Creed or Chaos?* Manchester, N.H.: Sophia Institute Press, 1996.

Torrance, Thomas F. *Preaching Christ Today: The Gospel and Scientific Thinking.* Grand Rapids: William B. Eerdmans, 1994.

Wainwright, Geoffrey. *For Our Salvation: Two Approaches to the Work of Christ.* Grand Rapids: William B. Eerdmans, 1997.

Willimon, William H. *The Service of God.* Nashville: Abingdon, 1979.